IT´S ALL RUGBY

*This book is dedicated to Leisha,
Michael and Johnathan, the reasons that
I've tried to keep moving forward*
xxx

Rick O'Shea

IT'S ALL RUGBY

with Alun Gibbard

y Lolfa

First impression: 2014

The publishers wish to acknowledge the support of
Cyngor Llyfrau Cymru

Cover design: Y Lolfa
Cover photograph: BBC

ISBN: 978 178461 007 4

Published and printed in Wales
on paper from well-maintained forests by
Y Lolfa Cyf., Talybont, Ceredigion SY24 5HE
website www.ylolfa.com
e-mail ylolfa@ylolfa.com
tel 01970 832 304
fax 832 782

Foreword by Gwyn Jones

RICK O'SHEA. THE man. The Life. The Legend. The man who's appetite for life is surpassed only by his appetite for curry. Rick and I have been friends for 15 years. We met when he took over the running of my local late-night haunt and we have spent endless nights talking nonsense since.

I'm not entirely sure how Rick went from being a cider-supping landlord to a media personality. But that's nothing compared to my amazement about how he then became a doctor.

During our highly intellectual late-night discussions at the Cameo, Rick and I would often discuss life's great philosophical questions. In one particularly long session I may have inadvertently suggested that Rick could do something in the world of broadcasting. A minor role obviously, but I didn't expect him to take up the idea, and I certainly didn't expect him to be any good at it. His success has shocked us both.

However, I will deny any suggestion that I either encouraged or supported Rick in pursuing his late career switch to medicine. I may have told him that he's clever and I may have said that medicine is a wonderful career. But any hint in this tome that I was in any way responsible for Rick O'Shea becoming your doctor is a slur on my good name.

Almost all of Rick's success is thanks to his long-suffering wife Leisha, who has endured the many changes in career that Rick has inflicted upon her. But, whatever he wanted to do next, Leisha continued to stand by him lovingly, cooking him food and buying him beer.

But despite his many inadequacies Rick is wonderful company, endlessly optimistic and a loyal friend. Many of my happiest memories have been those special occasions spent with Rick. Either singing along to *Les Misérables* at four in the morning, eating every variation of takeaway food possible over an Easter weekend (Leisha was away) or listening to his latest shaggy-dog story over a cup of tea.

I am honoured that Rick has asked me to write the foreword to this book (probably because I'm doing it for free) and I hope you get an insight into why it's such a pleasure to call him one of my one hundred closest friends. (You can swap that to 'one of my few close friends' if you want...)

1

THE SIX NATIONS. If you are of a certain age it doesn't get much bigger than that. It was once the only live rugby on telly, and it provided me with my first memories of the game I love. As a child exiled in Cornwall in the early 1970s, I sat with my mum and gran around the telly and cheered for Edwards et al., and boy, were they worth cheering for. In the intervening 40 years or so, nothing has diminished my love of this tournament, nothing at all... not even Wales being crap and getting humped by England!

Andy Williams may think that Christmas is the 'most wonderful time of the year' but for me it comes about seven weeks later.

That period of intense focus for every rugby fan north of Andorra and south of the Shetlands, brings out the deepest passion from the most vegetated armchair fan. And it's been happening for a long time. In 1883, Wales, England, Ireland and Scotland started to battle each other for the home nations' title. In 1910, France made it Five Nations, and Italy joined in 2000 to form the Six Nations we enjoy today. Wales has done pretty well in this latest incarnation of international rugby warfare – coincidentally ever since I've been working on *Scrum V* – and I have been so glad to be a small part of bringing that Six Nations competitive bite and energy to the small screen.

Take 2011, for example. My brief was simple: *Scrum V* deployed me on a fact-finding mission, to go to the games involving whoever Wales were playing next, and interview any relevant player or coach about how they saw their forthcoming fixture against Wales. It meant, of course, that I missed most of the games Wales played, but it certainly was a different way of being a part of the championship. That particular one didn't get off to a very good start, though. In the one game I did see Wales play, they lost to England on a Friday night. That's never a good feeling any day of the week. That was the first Friday night fixture ever in the history of the home nations' competition. First thing the following morning, I was on a plane to Paris to watch France play Wales' next opponents, Scotland.

I had pitch-side access during the game, which in itself was amazing, so I could ask questions if I needed to as the game went on. I was also told by my producer to ask some questions in the post-match press conference. As routine as these 'pressers' are, they can be quite intimidating. No one wants to ask the one stupid question that brings ridicule to your ears. I've played rugby and I played a bit of what they used to call 'first-class rugby' – I stress, a *bit*. I never played it to elite level and certainly not to international standard.

I always feel the need to give the person I'm interviewing – be it player or coach – the impression that I do know a bit about the game. The nature of this specific brief was made even more difficult because I was not there to ask questions about the game they'd just played, but one in the future, the one they weren't focused on in any way, shape or form at that particular moment. I did feel those pressures as I stepped into the gathering of rugby's finest journalists, waiting to interview some of the best international players.

In addition to all this, in the back of my mind, was the nightmare experience I had on my first ever TV appearance, some time in 2003. I'd been asked to conduct ringside interviews at the Welsh amateur boxing finals. (I can only assume a flu epidemic had broken out in Llandaf!) I refer you to my mantra of wanting to give the interviewee the feeling I knew what I was doing. However, I knew very little about boxing! My job at the Afan Lido that evening was to interview the winner of each fight. I cottoned on to a way of asking sensible questions to these boxers. Boxing champions, Nicky Piper and Colin Jones, were providing the main commentary. I would carefully listen to Nicky and Colin – and then ask questions using phrases I'd heard them use. So if they said that a particular boxer had his 'jab going very well', during the post-fight chat I'd open with, 'Congratulations Dai, great performance. You certainly had your jab going very well, didn't you?' Simple.

We had covered all the fights from the lowest weight up, and it was time for the final – the clash of the heavyweights. A big army man – I think his name was Justin Jones – was up against Welsh rugby international Byron Hayward, as handy in the ring as he was on the paddock. As I recall, this was a special fight for Byron. He was making his last appearance before having to retire from amateur boxing on the grounds of his age. It was quite an occasion for him then, the chance to retire as the Welsh amateur heavyweight champion. What a way to end his boxing career.

It didn't go very well. Jones was a formidable fighter and, even though Byron did quite well in the first round, he was knocked out cold in the second. I got ready to interview the winner, but the director of the outside broadcast, Geraint Rowlands, whispered in my earpiece, asking me to interview Byron as well. The fact that he was a rugby international and that he'd fought his last fight was reason enough to interview the loser on this occasion. I had no problem with that. I knew Byron from my rugby playing days and I felt a lot more comfortable going to talk to him.

When he'd come round sufficiently from his knocked-out state, I started with my first question:

'Byron, that was your last ever fight; it wasn't the fairy-tale ending you had hoped for. How do you think it went?'

Nooooo... What a stupid question!

Byron looked at me blankly. I could hear Rowlands laughing uncontrollably in my earpiece. I felt really dumb. Byron eventually managed to find some words, but all he could say was:

'Well... not very well really. He knocked me out.'

Bless him! I think I was trying to ask him where he thought it went wrong. But that's not what came out.

With echoes of the Afan Lido ringing in the back of my mind then, some eight years later I walked into a Six Nations press conference. I faced Scotland's Andy Robinson and Alastair Kellock and got through the whole thing unscathed. Great! Next up, the following week, was Italy versus England, as Wales were to face the Italians in their next game. I asked the Italy coach, Nick Mallett, some questions and it went OK. But what I remember from that occasion was Martin Johnson. Journalists can be a cynical bunch who have seen it all and done it all before. Nothing surprises them. The murmur and mumble of chat amongst them in the press room before Nick Mallett came in barely subsided once he entered. But, once Johnson stepped into the room, the whole place went quiet, as even the most seasoned rugby journalist was silent in respect, or awe, or fear, or possibly all three, for the giant who had just walked in. I hadn't seen that before. I didn't think it was possible for hacks to be affected in such a way. I could see why they'd reacted as they did. He has the most incredible presence. I almost expected some Darth Vader-type music to be played as he walked to the front of the room. I don't know if he actively intends to intimidate, he just does. That left quite an impression on me, one that would haunt me in a few short weeks.

My last mission on that Six Nations campaign was the Ireland versus England game in Dublin. It was a hectic weekend. On the Friday night I was speaking at a dinner in Cwmafan RFC with Steve Fenwick. When the dinner finished I was picked up by my producer Ceri Jenkins, and we made our way to Fishguard to catch the night ferry across to Ireland. The Dublin game was a Grand Slam showdown occasion, with England hoping for a Grand Slam and Ireland determined to spoil the party, while Wales were playing in Paris later that evening, still with an outside chance of the title.

Before going to Dublin, on the Thursday night, I was sat enjoying a drink at the Cameo Club in Cardiff with Gwyn Jones. During the evening conversation turned to the weekend, and the former Wales captain surprised me by saying that he hoped England would win. Clearly, I was stunned. I asked who he was, and what had he done with Gwyn Jones! He told me that, all nonsense aside, he felt that England had played the better rugby throughout the tournament. They had often chosen to be positive instead of pragmatic, often choosing to carry the ball rather than kick. And that is how they started the game against Ireland; through the hands they clocked up the phases moving left and right. But this was Dublin and this was Ireland; they rarely went forward and they were soon drawn into a scrap, for which they proved ill-equipped, losing 24–8. No Grand Slam for England then, even if they did finish at the top of the table.

After the game, it was my time to go to the press conference and ask Martin Johnson some questions. I had to face this intimidating man on the occasion of his team failing to achieve a Grand Slam which had been theirs for the taking. Basically, the Irish had pulled his pants down. Up in the stands, Ceri and I both agreed that to ask him how he thought Wales would do in the World Cup would be tantamount to suicide. I really wasn't up for that. Suddenly, in a light bulb moment, I remembered the conversation I had with Gwyn Jones at the Cameo Club. I decided to put it to the great man that perhaps he had actually been too ambitious for such a climactic showdown. That was it! I focused my mind, and recited the lines as I made my way to the 'presser'.

The room, crackling with anticipation of the gathering storm as I entered, was, in effect, a lecture theatre. There was a big 'top table' laden with microphones and recording devices. At the front the 'scribes' were assembled in the banks of seating that sloped up to the back of the room. I took my seat about halfway back, and waited.

Just as at Twickenham, the buzz of hacks filled the room, until Martin Johnson came in, of course. Then I swear the temperature dropped several degrees and the lights dimmed. First the old pros went at it, the rugby press heavyweights: Peter Jackson, Steve James, Stuart Barnes, Chris Foy, some bloke from Lydney (Ha! Take that, Jamer... not that you'll ever read this!).

There was a lull in the questioning, this was it. I couldn't put it off any longer... I put my hand up...

'Mr Johnson.'

He turned and looked me straight in the eyes...

Oh shit, I thought. My mind was racing... that's it, there's no going back now... OK, don't lose it Fatty, he's just a bloke... look him in the eyes, stick your chest out, speak up...

'Rick O'Shea, BBC Wales...'

'What are you doing here?'

The entire room erupted in laughter as everyone turned to look at me, just like a classroom of schoolboys would turn to laugh at the school dunce.

There was no hiding place. There was a little bit of an edge in there anyway, as all the others were scribes and I was the television man – always a friendly rivalry – I'm not even sure I should have been there, and Johnson's gag was grist to their mill.

I then had to work out where I would go next. What would I do? What would I say? But Johnson hadn't finished with me.

'You must be very high ranking in BBC Wales if they sent you here when Wales are playing in France!'

Cue even more uproarious laughter!

Many are the times since that I've wished I'd had the presence of mind to say, 'Gatland sent me to pick up the trophy and take it to Paris.' Or, 'Who do I see to get a refund on my England Grand Slam T-shirt?' and so on. But at the time, nothing came out.

I decided to persevere with my intended question, despite my little setback.

'I was speaking to Gwyn Jones this week and he told me that he hoped England would win the Grand Slam...'

'Oh please, don't be nice to me now!'

'... because you've played some great rugby during this campaign. Do you think you paid the price in this game for playing too much rugby?'

He furrowed that heavy brow of his and narrowed his eyes.

'It's all rugby, mate,' he said, pausing briefly. 'Winning a line-out on your own line and not conceding a scrum, not giving away a stupid penalty when you've just taken the lead, it's all rugby, it's all rugby isn't it?'

He wasn't being flippant. He was just saying it like it is – that you don't have to play like Wales did in the 1970s for it to be considered rugby. Everything that happens on the pitch is done in the name of rugby. That was his philosophy. I'd reached the end of my contribution to the press conference and, truth be told, I was chuffed. I'd got a question in and I'd stuck to the best piece of advice that I'd ever been given as an aspiring journalist, from the man I consider to be the consummate journalist, Eddie Butler.

'Rick,' he said, 'remember this, be loved or be hated, but never be ignored.'

They could not ignore that! For the next hour, my phone was buzzing with texts and calls, each one saying the same thing. Players, broadcasters, journalists alike, were all throwing this back at me, 'It's all rugby, mate'. Even Eddie himself chuckled away as we waited for the plane home the next morning.

Three days later I was live pitch-side at the end of the Welsh Varsity match between Cardiff and Swansea universities at the Millennium Stadium. Two famous Welsh students, Jamie Roberts and Gwyn Jones, joined me for a chat. I asked them, brimming with earnest enthusiasm, what they thought such an occasion would mean to the young students on the pitch. Gwyn's eyes sparkled with glee; his answer:

'Well, Rick… It's all rugby, mate!'

When the laughter and the leg-pulling had died down, and the dust had settled on my Johnson-gate experience, when I stop to think about it now, that throwaway phrase is actually so true and so relevant to me. My life has been all about rugby. I didn't play the game to a great standard. But that's the great thing about the game; you just don't have to play it to be a part of it, a part of the culture and heritage it generates. It gives you so much. The major turns in my life have been rugby-driven: my childhood, the jobs I've had, owning a club and a restaurant, the college course I did, playing the game, my broadcasting, even studying medicine – directly or indirectly, for me, it's all rugby.

2

ALL THAT BEING said, I have no illusions. This is not the memoir of a rugby-playing great. My dear friend and colleague, Phil Steele, often reminds me that I'm a very modest man given that I have plenty to be modest about! Unlike Phil, who played for Wales B and was, therefore, rather good, I've had a great life through being an average rugby player. That's what rugby can do for you.

That's why the Six Nations is such a self-fulfilling prophecy. It's the 'big show' for the common or garden rugby man or woman. The results are largely irrelevant. Often to the chagrin of rugby's fundamentalist wing, a Six Nations weekend is simply the greatest social gathering. It's all things to all people. It's a weekend 'tour' with a game in the morning; it's a stag do or a hen do; it's folk getting together once a year, or every two years, or once a decade. It is an occasion that builds memories and galvanises relationships – it can even end a few. The whole of rugby life, from the grassroots up, is there. It's the reward for what we do every weekend – the Six Nations is the crowning glory.

In time, the World Cup may well achieve the same status, and be an event that feeds our recollections, our social memories, and our nostalgia. But it still won't have what the Six Nations has, because the World Cup only happens once every four years.

It has often been stated that I have the perfect face for radio. I never dreamt that anyone would put me in front of a camera. Despite this obvious handicap, I have carved out a niche. If I have any ability as a broadcaster – and there are plenty who question this – it is perhaps that those who watch and play rugby can see a little bit of themselves in me. I hope that they can see that I love the game. I get to do what any rugby fan would love to do, and I try to do it with a smile on my face. Yes, of course, it's all rugby. It does matter. But it matters only for that moment in time. It's just a game, and that 'time' passes. This attitude is not unique, this spirit that's in me is in every other rugby fan, especially in Wales – it's second nature. It's like breathing.

It's not something that I've grown to love as my life went on. I was born into it. My dad, John O'Shea, played on the tight-head for Wales on five occasions in the late 1960s. He was at school with John Dawes – Lewis School, Pengam – and he went on to play for Cardiff, before being chosen to play for Wales and then the British and Irish Lions on their tour of South Africa in 1968. He played for the Lions in the first Test against the Springboks, in the same team as Gareth Edwards, Barry John, Gerald Davies and Willie John McBride. He's a Test Lion, my dad, and that is an exclusive club. I'm very proud of him. But, he formed an even more exclusive club a couple of weeks later when he became the first and, at the time writing, only Lion to be sent off for fighting! I'm very, very proud of my dad!

He was playing in the game against Eastern Transvaal, after the second Test. He'd been dropped for that Test, which he has later admitted was the right decision, as he had not played well enough. That Eastern Transvaal game has gone down as one of those particularly dirty games, 'The Battle of Springs' as it's referred to affectionately. About six years ago, dad was asked to write his version of that particular battle in a rugby book, *Tales from the Back of the Bus*. With some possibly misplaced paternal faith in my journalistic abilities, he sent it to me to check over before publication. I am happy to say that I had little to add.

As an after-dinner speaker I rarely tell this story – it's dad's story and not mine to tell – but it's a cracking yarn and worth including as a little piece of British Lions history. So here it is in his own words:

Saturday, 29 June 1968 – a day that is written in rugby history, sadly for all the wrong reasons, for it was the day that I became the first, and thus far the only British Lion to be sent from the field and remain there.

I had been picked to play at tight-head prop for the match on the high veldt against Eastern Transvaal, in a town called Springs.

The portents were not good; a year earlier on the same ground France had played Eastern Transvaal in a brutal match that required the referee to blow early to avoid further bloodshed.

In the wake of that match, one of the Eastern Transvaal players, if my memory serves me correctly, a flanker named Britz, had been suspended *sine die* (a little Welsh phrase meaning 'not likely to play again').

However, with the Lions in town, he was granted a permit to play and a party of hunters was sent into the bush to capture the flanker and bring him back to Springs.

As expected, the match was a bad-tempered affair, punctuated by skirmishes that forced the referee, Bert Woolley, to issue a general warning to the forwards regarding foul play, promising that the next man to offend would get his marching orders.

Early in the second period our half-back, Roger Young, followed his opposite number around a scrum and, as he did, Britz attacked him, and, as I was on the tight-head, it happened right in front of me. I took exception, and immediately intervened on Roger's behalf.

This was a BIG mistake because, while I was avenging this despicable act, Eastern Transvaal scored their only try. I found myself engaged with a number of the opposition in what might be described as some sort of 'fisticuffs', although I may add that I would be guaranteed to come second in any two-man boxing match.

Mr Woolley, who had been temporarily distracted by the act of awarding a try, was presented with this scenario and made a summary decision.

'Number 3, OFF! Number 3, OFF!'

It seemed to echo around the stadium as the referee called out. Naturally, being a prop forward, I wasn't sure what number I was wearing. I asked one of the wingers (they always carry a programme) and he confirmed that I was wearing number 3.

Desperation was now setting in to such an extent that I turned to Delme Thomas, one of our second rowers. He asked me where I was going and I said I was going off.

'Why, are you tired?' he asked.

'No,' I said. 'The ref's sent me off.'

I was now in panic mode, and so was Delme. He suspected that if I went off he'd be moved up to tight-head. He suggested that I go behind the posts with him for the conversion, hoping that because the opposition had just scored a try the referee might forget my misdemeanour.

Now front rowers don't put much store to a lot of what second rowers tell them, like, 'I promise I'll push in the next scrum', but this seemed a good plan at the time. Sadly, Mr Woolley proved to have a remarkable memory for a referee and once again delivered his sentence:

'Number 3, OFF!'

Delme's last words to me as I headed off were, 'I think you are right Tess! I'll see you after the game.'

This was the beginning of the end. As I approached the touchline the crowd erupted and started throwing a variety of objects at me, including seat covers and large oranges with knobs on, which I believe are called 'naartjies'.

Throughout the tour we had noticed these oranges on sale outside the grounds, but we had never actually seen anyone eating them. It occurred to me they might have been waiting for a British Lion to be sent off so that they could throw them at him, and I can understand why South Africa produces so many good extra-cover fielders, because most of them hit me.

There was worse to come! As I was about to leave the

field, a well-dressed gentleman came through the gate and approached me with his hand out. I thought he wanted to shake my hand in consolation, but instead he closed his fist and struck me on the jaw.

Fortunately for me, I was escorted to safety by Ronnie Dawson, our assistant manager; Tony Horton, Haydn Morgan, a 1962 Lion now living in South Africa; and a number of South African police.

Unfortunately for my assailant, Willie John McBride jumped over the fence, took him in a headlock and pointed out the error of his ways, an act for which I'll always be in his debt.

The Lions won the game with 14 men, 37 points to 9, which probably meant they played a lot better without O'Shea than with him.

My assailant was charged with assault by the South African police. I was told that he had stated in his defence the reason he hit me: it was a very hot day and the toilet facilities at Springs were very poor. I'm still not sure what he thought I was. He received a 200 Rand fine.

They say that out of adversity great things can be achieved, that was certainly the case on this occasion. After my departure from the field, the management sent a message to the dressing rooms via Keith Jarrett.

'Get dressed as quickly as you can and take your place in the grandstand next to the Lions management. And hold your head up.'

On arrival at the after-match reception, my team-mates told me to lead them into the room, to show I had their support.

Although the judicial hearing had not been held at this stage, management selected me for the next game against Northern Transvaal, a selection that should have gone to Tony Horton. This decision also indicated management's support.

Because of the stand taken by management, the crowd behaviour, the assailant, and a favourable report from the referee, I received a severe reprimand, and took my place in the team as selected.

J.B.G. Thomas, the leading sports writer of the *Western Mail*, took me aside at the team reception and introduced me to Bert Woolley, whom he had met when Woolley brought a South African Schoolboys' cricket team to Wales.

I offered my apologies and said I understood his decision to send me off.

We kept in touch and even exchanged Christmas cards for a while. In fact, 11 years later, Woolley, in an interview with a South African newspaper, stated that under the current laws involving touch judges, 'he would not have sent O'Shea off' on that fateful day in Springs. Just a bit late!

It's over 40 years on now, and I've recently attended the reunion of our Lions team in London.

The game has moved on, as have we all. Rules have changed; for example, in our day lifting was illegal and an art – now it's compulsory.

In 1968 I was awarded the honour of being a member of a British Lions side, a side which included players who would go on to become legends of the game of rugby and, 40 years later, at our reunion in London, to be with these lads again proved that, long after the games are forgotten, the special spirit and friendship was stronger than ever.

Rugby union and my fellow team members have given me a gift that is priceless, and for that I shall be eternally grateful.

There is a slight technical detail to be made about his account. He isn't actually the first player to be sent off for the Lions. He is the first to be sent off for foul play. Dennis Dobson of England, over 100 years ago, was sent off for using 'indecent language', later downgraded to 'an improper expression' which could be described as a technical offence. Dad still has the honour of being the first to be sent off for punching someone!

Dad tasted the rarified atmosphere of the elite; he was a recipient of that rugby gift. I may never have soared so high, but I share that eternal gratitude, even if for very different reasons. It comes from the same place. It was passed down to me, in the blood.

* * *

It all began for me on 9 January 1968 at St Joseph's Nursing Home, in the Malpas area of Newport. I tend to keep that quiet, by virtue of the fact that dad, of course, played for and captained Cardiff, and was of the persuasion that the only good thing to come from Newport was the road to Cardiff!

My grandparents on dad's side used to run the workingmen's club in Oakdale. My granddad was also called Richard, and I'm named after him. They had previously run many pubs in the Newport area, and Caerleon. But when the Second World War bombs started to fall and cause some damage to Newport and the surrounding area, they moved to England, which is where dad was actually born. He keeps that quiet, too! They didn't go far from Newport though, only across the water to Portishead, near Bristol. They didn't stay there long either, and were soon back on Welsh soil.

A few years later, my father's dad died very young; I believe it was from TB. Again it's a bit sketchy, but I also believe that the powers that be wouldn't allow my grandmother to run the Oakdale workingmen's club as a woman on her own, and so she had an opportunity to return to Caerleon. My dad at this time, however, was already in school, and his mother had no plans to move him because Lewis School, Pengam, was a very good one. The problem was solved by a family that has come to mean as much to me as my own.

While at Pengam my dad became best friends with a young man named Chris Padfield. To say they were close, both on and off the pitch, would be no exaggeration – dad was a prop; Chris, the hooker! I'm not entirely certain of the circumstances, but the long and short of it is that Chris' mum, Zena, whose heart was a big as the Islwyn borough she went on to be mayoress of, 'took my dad in' and looked after him as her own. I know that Zena and her husband Bill's kindness had a profound effect on him – so much so that my father, born a Catholic, converted to the Church of Wales out of respect to the family that had helped him so much.

I never met Bill, as he passed away before I was born, but I knew and loved 'Auntie' Zena and her second husband, 'Uncle Reg'. My word, she was formidable woman. Chris has clearly inherited all of his mother's kindness, and then some more. To this day I have never met a nicer, more generous man. He also boasted a fine career in rugby, playing for Newbridge and Ebbw Vale, and went on to coach them both, as well as the Cardiff team that beat the Wallabies in 1975.

O'Shea and Padfield were a formidable unit in a formidable team that included many fine players, including John Dawes and Dennis Hughes. Dad and Chris had their caps for Welsh Schoolboys together. There was no separating Chris and dad after Lewis School, either. They both went on to St Luke's College to do teacher training together. They didn't leave at the same time, however. Dad got kicked out early!

He started to work for Heinz, and then got a job as a brewery rep, just about the same time as he started to play for Cardiff, from 1963 until he retired in 1970. He was capped three times in 1967 and twice in 1968, the year he played for the Lions. The Battle of the Springs, however, probably cost him his international career.

He toured South Africa three years running during that time: with Cardiff in 1967, the Lions in 1968, and with the Barbarians in 1969. Yes, they did let him back in! In fact, dad had much better luck on the Dark Continent than the other member of the 'naughty Lions club'. Dennis Dobson, when posted to Nyasaland as a colonial officer, was fatally gored by a charging rhino! Thus prompting his old housemaster at Oxford to comment that he always had a weak hand off! It's all rugby!

'Behind every great man is a great woman' goes the saying. Although I might be accused of bias, there is no greater a woman than my mam! My mum's family came from Newport. Her dad, Joe Wilde, after whom I was given my middle name Joseph, was an engineer, and I believe quite an athlete in his youth – tennis was his sport, another gift that has skipped the generations! My nan, Mavis Chave, was originally from Llandeilo, and was a Welsh speaker in her youth before moving to Newport. In later years my grandparents ran a chip shop in Commercial Road, in the Pill area. Mum attended the convent school that was located in the building now known as Tredegar House, a National Trust managed mansion by now.

I lived in Hafodyrynys, a village between Pontypool and Crumlin in the old county of Gwent, until I was about two years old. While dad was playing for Cardiff, he worked as a brewery rep for the famous Courage company. He was doing very well indeed. That is no surprise to anyone who knows him, as he is such a raconteur and the funniest man I know. Call me biased again, but I think that's true.

So when he hung up his rugby boots, he was given promotion to manage a team of reps based in Cornwall. We moved as a family to Penzance. I don't remember a great deal, if anything, about growing up during my first two years in Wales, but I do remember the legacy of Acre Close in Hafodyrynys. My godmother, Janet Angel, lived opposite us, with my 'Uncle' Elwyn and 'Nanna' Smith living right next door. Nanna wasn't related to me in any way, but despite us moving away to Cornwall, and her having about 15 of her own grandchildren, she still sent me £5 on my birthday every year until she died when I was about 17. I think that tells you all you need to know about Valleys people.

Dad dusted down his boots when we got to Penzance and

played a few games for the Penzance & Newlyn team, the Pirates. But dad didn't stay in Cornwall for long. Courage had plans, big plans. They wanted to break into the Australian market. A bold venture indeed, as lager is the amber nectar that pumps through Aussie veins. But that's what Courage wanted to do. They put a team together to attack the brewery world of Oz, and knowing how much the Aussies loved sport, they felt that dad should be in that team. Mum and I went with him when he set sail for Australia. A new adventure lay ahead of us.

We set up home in the suburbs of Melbourne. Apparently, it was just like life in *Neighbours*, but maybe with a little bit more space between the houses! For all the sun however, and the golden glow of Australian life, I think it was quite difficult for mum to settle. She was a Valleys girl, a million miles from home, family and friends. She agreed to the move because dad's involvement was only a secondment, due to last about 18 months or two years. Sadly for mum, my granddad died not long after we arrived. That was a pretty good reason to go back home. Courage was prepared pay for our trip back to the UK, but not for the passage back to Australia again, which provided a good reason not to return.

We'd kept our home in Cornwall and mum decided to stay there, with dad scheduled to return when his secondment finished. My grandmother, now a widow, came from Wales to live with us.

Dad was as capable a rep as he was a prop, and soon other avenues opened up for him when the Courage contract came to an end. He felt that they were too good opportunities to miss. He would come home every year and we would go out there every other year, or so. There was, however, no way that their marriage could be sustained over such distance and time. With hindsight, you might say that it was inevitable

25

that they would separate, but I don't recall any sense of that. Our life seemed perfectly normal. Dad's visits home were regular and exciting, and trips to Australia in the 1970s were quite simply the most wonderful adventures. They did not divorce until I was 16 years old.

I've since had many a conversation with dad about that period, especially since I've become a father myself. I've been more than curious to know how he felt being on the other side of the world from his family. Despite the geography, he's had a huge influence on my life, and I respect him immensely. I do wonder if that's because of his status in my consciousness as a bit of a hero. It can't have been easy to be so far away from his family.

For my mum and me, of course, it meant quite a different family life. We settled back in Mousehole and I got on with my Cornish upbringing. This put me in a fairly unique situation. As an O'Shea I had Irish heritage, I'd been born in Wales, and brought up in England – that's three countries I wasn't good enough to play for!

3

MUM, NAN AND I settled down to live in Mousehole. I defy anyone to find me a prettier village anywhere. If you were a Hollywood director looking for an archetypal picture postcard fishing village, Mousehole is where you'd go. It has two granite quays, an island off its shore, and it's composed of traditional fishermen's cottages that tumble down the hillside virtually into the sea. On the hills farmers work the soil, looking down to the water where fishermen make their living.

The ocean, therefore, opened out in front of us, and the land stretched up behind us. In between the cottages, a couple of cracking pubs added their own architectural punctuation. That famous Welsh poet and frequent pub visitor, Dylan Thomas, described it as 'the loveliest village in England'. He married Caitlin at the registry office in Penzance, and they were frequent visitors to The Ship in Mousehole during that visit to Cornwall. I'm not sure if it's still there – I think Cyril Torrie might have annexed it – but there was once a 'Dylan's corner' in The Ship, long after he left both the area and this mortal coil.

Frequenting The Ship was a tradition that I felt I needed to keep. It became my local, and I spent many, many a night there – some of which became mornings – enjoying Mike and Tracy Maddern's hospitality and, of course, the banter of the rest of the village. I particularly recall one epic night following a party to celebrate a 'refurb' of the pub, around 1990. It was Christmas, and by this stage my mum had become postmistress of the village, buying the local post office to ensure that she could put me through university. This meant that during the holidays I'd get some work as a relief postman, helping the regular postmen, Barry Cornish and John Drew, with the heavy mail.

The evening had been a belter, full of laughter and songs and possibly a very badly performed haka! I vaguely remember saying to Mike, 'Right I've got to go, I'm delivering the post in the morning.'

As I pulled open the heavy oak door which kept the gales out – as well as daylight – I discovered that the sun was already up and Barry Cornish had started his round, informing me, as he marched past, that my mum was not best pleased!

I rushed back full apologies and good intentions, grabbed the sack and headed off on the more arduous leg of the round. I was later found in an acutely confused state, slumped in a hedge halfway up Raginnis Hill! This episode earned me the nickname, Postman Fat, one of many monickers that I've picked up along the way. Anyway, that was an aside. I didn't go to The Ship when I was three years old, honest!

I needed to go to school, however, and that happened in Penzance, at St Erbyn's School – a fantastic place that enjoyed a great tradition. The school was opened by a certain Miss B. M. Steadman in 1918 and it was she who gave it the name St Erbyn, in honour of what she called a true Cornish saint. But I wonder how true he was, because there's a record of a St Erum who was referred to by an alias, St Erbyn. Why would a saint need an alias?

The school grew quite quickly from those early days and, by 1926, it was a boys' preparatory school. The following year it was sold to a man who had more of a statement than a name – Reginald Frederick d'Argaville Carr! Luckily, he was happy for people to call him plain Rex! The school grew under his guidance and, in 1935, girls were re-admitted to the school, when Rex's daughter Bridget joined. During the Second World War the boarding side closed down. A few years later, numbers were up to double the pre-war figures, but now with day pupils only. Mike Jenkin joined in the late 1950s, became a junior partner in 1962, and took over as headmaster in 1970 when Rex retired. Mike Jenkin, a former Oxford Blue, was the man in charge when I joined, and the first of several rugby men to have a profound influence on me. I remember seeing the school building for the first time, a great ivy-clad, stone presence in Clarence Street, with playing fields at the back.

I look back on that education now with fondness. Academically, it gave me a broad foundation: I was taught Latin, French, History, Geography and similar subjects from the age of about nine. In my last year there, before going on to secondary school, we did the sciences. I remember going on Saturday mornings in my final year to the grammar school where the Physics, Chemistry and Biology teachers would teach us the basics. They would obviously have been paid privately to teach us those lessons.

I sat my 11-plus exam. For the uninitiated, or the young, that was an entrance exam to determine which secondary school you went to, either the grammar school if you passed, or the secondary modern if you didn't. A lifelong track record of variable exam results began with success – I passed the 11-plus and the Humphry Davy Grammar School beckoned. It was a great old school, named after a great local hero, the famous scientist who grew up in Penzance and invented many things, most notably the miners' safety lamp.

I was only there for one year. No, I wasn't kicked out. Then, just as now, the education system was a political football, and the grammar schools were being phased out. By

my second year at Humphry Davy Grammar School, it had
become plain old Humphry Davy School. Whatever the label
attached to the school, it brought together the bright lights
of Penwith, the county borough that unifies all points west
of Hayle and St Ives to Land's End. Lots of my classmates
from St Erbyn's went on to the public schools of the West
Country: Truro School, Kelly College, Millfield, Sherbourne
etc. I, therefore, had a massive advantage over the local boys
coming from the county primary schools, who were doing
French, Latin, the sciences and the like, for the first time. I'd
already been taught those subjects for a couple of years, so
it didn't stretch me. But I really enjoyed my time there. I can
still remember the school song:

> King Arthur ruled in Lyonesse, a mighty Christian King
> His Knights the flower of chivalry as ancient poets sing
> And since his days all men may praise full many a Cornish name
> That shine securely as the lamp where glistens Davy's fame...
> Godolphin, St Aubyn, Trelawny and Treneere
> Come sing together and a song that all the world may hear
> The heroes of the Cornish past with pride we may recall
> Our school be still the first and last
> Our motto 'One and All'!

Not only is it a cracking old song, it's also an example of my
uncanny ability to remember stuff of very little consequence.
But it's important to me. I can do all of 'American Pie', too!

School to me was rugby, cricket and friends, occasionally
interrupted by lessons. In my year the rugby team was really
very good. It's easy to recall the team because it hardly
changed over the five years:

1. Adrian Rutter
2. Tony Hands
3. Paul Osborne

4. Stephen Ward
5. Phil Rich
6. Paul Bergen
7. Ian Luke
8. Simon Humphreys
9. Richard O'Shea (I know… more of this later!)
10. Billy Peters (captain)
11. David Coneybeare
12. Tim Boston
13. Gordon Maddern
14. Simon Rowe
15. Richard Brownfield

In the first five years at school we were only beaten twice. Sadly, both times in the County Cup, which we competed for in years two to four. We lost to Camborne School in the semi-final in the second year, and Penair in Truro in the semi of the fourth year.

It was a golden era! In the early years our tactics were really simple – we just needed to get the ball to Simon Rowe, who was stupidly quick. If not put clean through – which he was, more often than not – he would then embark on that famous old technique employed by so many 12 year olds: he'd run backwards, away from tacklers, and across the field until he outpaced everyone and scored in the corner, possibly having traversed the pitch three times!

We grew as a team, though, as the years went by, and we had A* players. One was Billy Peters, a cracking number 10 with a great boot and a ridiculous sidestep. I will always remember his father Ted, a fantastic man, following us to every single game; he never missed one. He was a harsh critic of Billy, but Billy rarely gave him the opportunity to be too scathing. He was a great player who eventually starred in Cornwall's famous defeat of Yorkshire in the county championship final at Twickenham in 1991. Billy and I were the Edwards and John of Cornish schools' rugby in the early 1980s!

And, like those two, our relationship did not get off to the best of starts. Billy was from and played for St Ives; I was from and played for Penzance. Think Neath and Aberavon, or Newport and Cardiff, and you get the picture.

When we were first paired together in the first-year trials, I asked, 'Are you my fly-half?'

'I'm not *your* anything, pal!'

He had a sharp wit, was very clever, ridiculously handsome, incredibly athletic, with an unfeasible capacity for crap food, and yet, stayed in great nick! He was a real pain in the arse. We became great friends.

He was also the number one tennis seed in the school, although this was a shallow pool, as evidenced by the fact that I was the number two seed! Again, that was probably due to St Erbyn's, as there was a tennis court at that school, an unusual facility at a primary school. Even more unusual was the fact that, at primary age, we played croquet in school as well!

But more than anything, more than tennis or rugby, I think that St Erbyn's gave me an education not found on any curriculum. In a nutshell, I was academically very lazy. This wasn't helped by the fact that the first two years at Humphry Davy turned out to be so straightforward and not challenging in any way. I could breeze through these first two years, and I did. That did not set me up very well for the later years of comprehensive education. I did what I had to, enough to get me by. But no more.

Mousehole was, and probably remains in my conscience, home. We lived initially in one – and eventually three – of those lovely little cottages that I've described: 1, 2 and 3 Gurnick Cottages, Gurnick Street, Mousehole.

My mum was, and remains, the most amazing hostess. She was made a shrewd offer by Graham Curnow, the owner of the Regent Hotel in Penzance, to become its manageress. It was no coincidence, therefore, that between 1972 and 1979 (when Graham sold the Regent), it was 'the venue of choice' for every Welsh rugby team that toured Cornwall. Be it Crawshays or Cardiff, Tredegar or Ebbw Vale, they all knew my mum from her time as John O'Shea's wife on the circuit in Wales. She was extremely popular with these teams because she knew how to keep them happy – she would never shut the bar! As a consequence, the fire extinguishers were never set off, the fish pond never swum in! She would always maintain that 'the boys' would only ever get up to mischief if they did not have access to beer! If they had access to that, then they would drink until they fell asleep. As a hotel with a residents' licence, this was not a problem!

I swear that when I attend a rugby dinner in south Wales, as many people tell me that they've stayed at the Regent and ask after my mum, as claim that they've played against my dad! Well, almost as many!

Once again you can accuse me of bias but, like my dad, I'm incredibly proud of my mum; she was so much more than simply John O'Shea's wife. She is a warm and generous soul who is at her best in a crowd. She quickly established herself on the social scene in Penzance. She immersed herself in the rugby club, especially the mini-junior section. She was heavily involved in the sailing club and also the 'Vixens', the ladies' branch of the Western Hunt. Her connections in the brewery game meant that no matter what was happening in Mousehole – be it the regatta or carnival in summer, or the switching on of Christmas lights in winter – there was always a keg of beer hooked up and pumping in Gurnick Cottages.

Mousehole at that time wasn't what it is now: the 'second home' capital of the West Country. The tourists hadn't arrived in their coach loads then – well they had, but they rented the cottages then, they hadn't started to buy them. Cornwall was always a draw – if you pardon the pun – for artists. One celebrated Cornish artist, Jack Pender, was a friend of my mum's. He was born in Mousehole in the same year that St Erbyn's was established, and became a well-known artist, with his work shown in several public collections. The art community is very strong throughout the county by now, with Mousehole being its central point.

When I was growing up, Mousehole was a village full of locals: fishermen, farmers, pub landlords, teachers, shopkeepers – characters one and all. Now there's an education for you! It was very much like the Welsh communities we would associate with places like the Rhondda, or most of the Valleys, come to that. And just as descriptions of the Rhondda and the like have appeared to be either stereotypical, sentimental, or both, it's easy for me to make my childhood days sound like that, too. But really, we didn't lock the doors to our houses, everyone was in and out of each others' houses all the time. It was great! We played football on the beach every night until about ten o'clock, for as long as the light would allow. Every kid in the village had a little boat, just like kids would have bikes everywhere else. They were only ten-foot punts, but we all had one, and we would go out together to the harbour to mess about in them. We had bikes as well, of course.

A new family moved into the village when I was about 11, the Wheelers. They had two boys, Andy, and Matthew, known as 'Miffy'. Andy was about 18, and his brother, 15.

They sort of took me under their wing, even though they were the new boys. I was an only child; I still am, in fact! So I was on my own quite a bit, a little bit of a lost soul at times, I'm sure. I'd been to the private school in town, not the primary in the village. That made me a little bit more of an outsider, but none of this was to the point of being a loner in any way. I had lots of friends. I still have many of the friends from those early days in Cornwall. But Andy and Miffy seemed to adopt me. I was quite happy with that. They had an 18-foot boat, with an inboard motor and cabin! Better still, they were trained scuba divers and their dad was a scuba diving instructor. I was taught to dive in this way by them, and that too was an invaluable education. It was tremendously exciting to get up at six o'clock in the morning to go out on the water with them during the hazy days of the summer of 1980, with the first year of Humphry Davy Grammar School behind me.

Some days we would go out to fish with long lines; other days we'd shoot nets and go back the next day to pull them in. At least, I think we did, because the truth is I was bloody useless at any of the technical requirements of being a working fisherman, which is an incredibly difficult skill. God knows why they let me hang around with them, much less (in the traditional manner of a working fishing boat) give me a share of their 'catch'! It might only have been £5 or so, but that would go quite far in those days. So, once back on dry land, we would go to The Coastguard, a massive pub with landscaped gardens going down to the water. Andy was a university student, and looked like a young James Hunt; he was able to charm the barmaids to such an extent that he sneaked my first pint of Stella Artois out to me. The education continued... I owe them a huge debt!

Therefore, there was no shortage of distractions. Add to

this the distinct lack of any academic challenge at Humphry Davy for the first two years, and it comes as no surprise that things started to slip a bit scholastically by the third year. Everyone had started to catch me up and then overtake me. The curriculum was new. It was a level playing field for us all now, whatever primary education we'd received. By the fourth year, I was way off the pace. I was entered for nine O Levels; I got two.

I consider this to be a reasonable effort given that during my O Level summer in 1984, I had one eye on a trip to Sydney to visit my dad, and I was also engrossed in the cricket Test series between an England team (containing Ian Botham and David Gower) and that incredible West Indian team. I passed Geography and History, probably because there were still some St Erbyn's fumes left in the tank somewhere!

St Erbyn's gave me a really good grounding. It made me interested in all sorts of things, it made me well read. It also gave me my first rugby experiences. Mike Jenkin, as I've already mentioned, had a rugby Oxford Blue. No way was he not going to pass on his love of the game to us. I played in the school rugby team. The fact that we had such a team, in what was in effect our primary school, was in itself unusual. There was no age-grade rugby. No county primary school would have a team. As a result, we only ever played against two other private schools, Truro Cathedral School and Treliske. Mike Jenkin also made sure that anyone in the first XV would be given the opportunity to watch the Varsity match every year.

St Erbyn's is now closed. A block of flats stands where we received our education. The playing fields where we played rugby, football and cricket, are now a car park. To this day, whatever the circumstance, I will never, ever park my car in that car park. I would rather park on the outskirts of town and walk in. It's a matter of principle for me now. That's where I played rugby for the first time ever. It's where I scored my first try. It's where I took my first stumping as a wicketkeeper. It's where I first learned about values, rules and the good things in life – even if I didn't like my chocolate brown school uniform that much! We were taught really old-fashioned values – at least, that's what they would be called today. If we saw the mother of another pupil in town, we had to doff our caps to her. We had to open doors for our elders. They were nice values and they taught me respect. I just have such affection for that time that it seems wrong that I should ever park my car on the grounds where it all happened.

I will never ever forget what Mike Jenkin wrote in the headmaster's section of my last school report from St Erbyn's. He was broadly very complimentary, mostly of my sporting achievements – in my last year I'd won the rugby and cricket fielding cups (I took six stumpings in a match against Truro Cathedral School!). The last sentence, however, haunted me throughout my adult life as I grew to understand what he meant when he wrote: 'Richard has the "big match" potential, but I do wonder if he will ever put himself in a position to be picked.'

4

MOST CHILDREN WHO went to St Erbyn's were the sons and daughters of local doctors, butchers or businessmen. My best friend there, who ended up being my best man later in life, Anthony Stevenson, was the son of a man who owned a local fishing fleet. Another very close and dear friend was Steve Cary – his father was the skipper of a fishing boat called *The Diligent*. Fishermen are honourable men in communities such as Mousehole and Penzance. It's a dangerous job, deep-sea fishing, and that danger and closeness to the elements, often in the eye of a storm, creates a community that's got nothing to do with geography. It's very much like the mining communities of Wales, where a dangerous living pulls people together in a close bond not known by those on the outside. In Mousehole I was allowed to be a part of this community; I was allowed into its warp and weft. But I could never know it as they did, and feel it in the blood. I'm just glad I could experience as much as I did, and that I was a part of it for as long as I was.

The nature of such a community – its strength and vulnerability – became clear in 1981. That was the year in which Mousehole, by virtue of the Penlee lifeboat, entered the vocabulary of UK disasters which have led to loss of life and shattered communities.

This is a chapter that I have struggled to address; this was a terrible tragedy and one that I do not want to overly dramatise or overstate my role in. However, it remains an incredible episode that I feel I must relate, if only to pay tribute to those involved: most importantly to John

Blewett, the father of another very close friend of mine, Andrew Blewett, for whom I would act as best man later in life, but who at that time was an 11-year-old schoolboy. John Blewett was an impressive figure. Well over six feet tall, and a handsome man of few words unless something needed saying. He was a British Telecom's engineer, a man who could turn his hand to all sorts of practical skills. It would be hard to explain just how important his family was to me. In many ways, there was a parallel here between the Blewetts and the Padfields. My mum, like my dad's mum, worked very unsociable hours in the hospitality industry. It would be over-egging the pudding to say that they adopted me, but they often found this strange little Welsh boy sat at their dining table.

I learned that if I called for Andrew on the way to catch the school bus ten minutes before he was ready, his mum Caroline, another one of the amazingly kind people who have blessed my life, would pull up a chair and offer me tea and toast. This tactic was equally fruitful in the evenings, too! And so if I'd rock up 20 minutes before 'play time', I'd often be invited to join the family for supper!

If the weather was crap and we couldn't go out, I'd huddle up with the Blewetts in their living room. I vividly remember watching shows like *Top of the Pops* and *The Young Ones* until about nineish, when it was time for me to go home and time for John to pop down to The Ship!

John loved his rugby and played for the Pirates. He would ferry Andrew and I to and from training and sometimes, if I was playing for Humphry Davy after school, particularly on the pitches at St Clare with their old granite changing rooms, I would see John filling the doorway of that old shed, his collar turned up against the wind, and puffing on a smoke! As I said, I'm not trying to build up my part here – there was no mentor-pupil relationship between John and I – but he was a kind man who had come to watch me play. If ever I needed firm words from a male figure, it would be John that would say those words and I would listen. He was simply my best friend's father, but he was an influential figure in my early teenage years, nevertheless.

As beautiful as Mousehole is – it is after all at the far west of the country, jutting out into the ocean – it does get some terrible storms. There was a lifeboat based at Penlee Point, a quarter of a mile or so from Mousehole, and hence it was called the Penlee lifeboat. As 1981 was drawing to a close, a particularly bad storm hit the Cornish coastline. I was in Andrew's house at the time because it was his sister Sarah's birthday. I had a massive 13-year-old's crush on her and was more than happy to be asked along to the party!

I do remember it being a really bad night. We were more than used to wild storms and heavy seas, with the waves breaking on the quay wall and throwing spray over it. That was part and parcel of life in a Cornish fishing village. That night, however, the waves themselves swamped the south quay. We knew it was very bad.

The party was well under way, and the phone rang and John was called away to join the lifeboat – a normal enough occurrence for any one of the army of volunteers who run the lifeboats. On this occasion, the coaster, *Union Star*, was in trouble out at sea in the storm – its engines had failed completely. Just after ten past eight that evening, the lifeboat, the *Solomon Browne*, was launched to rescue the crew of the *Union Star*. Eight men were on board the lifeboat: coxswain Trevelyan Richards, second coxswain/mechanic and my next-door neighbour Stephen Madron, assistant mechanic Nigel Brockman, crew members Charlie Greenhaugh, Kevin

Smith, Barrie Torrie and Gary Wallis, and, of course, my friend Andrew's dad, emergency mechanic John Blewett. Being an engineer with BT meant that he was a valuable member of the crew, as he knew so much about engines and all things technical.

I was still at his house when the lifeboat hit the waves. I was enjoying the party; we were 13 and 14 year olds at a birthday celebration, and that was our world that night. Out at sea, in horrendous weather conditions, the *Solomon Browne* made several attempts to get alongside the *Union Star*. They succeeded in getting four people from the coaster and onto the lifeboat – the captain's wife and two teenage stepdaughters, as well as one of the crew members – they were apparently safe. A message was sent from the lifeboat to say, 'we've got four off'. But they were the last words anyone heard from any of the 12 on board the *Solomon Browne*. Later, they were all taken by the cruel sea.

The village was shaken to the core of its very existence. I didn't see what happened, but I did feel the emotional impact the disaster had on our little village. My best friend's dad, who'd been so good to me personally, went from his daughter's birthday party (where I was sat on the stairs watching him leave) and never came back.

I left Sarah's party with Tim Yendell, another old friend from school. He was staying at my house that weekend. The walk home was no more than 150 yards. It was a foul night. In the morning my mum came to my bedroom with a look on her face that I had never seen before. She told me that the lifeboat was lost at sea and, worse than that, the reports were that she was lost with all hands. I felt heavy. But I couldn't understand the enormity of the situation, even when it was confirmed that no one would come back alive.

This very small community village had lost eight men and

it had lost its lifeboat which in itself was a source of great pride as it had been involved in so many successful rescues, and was a part of local culture and folklore. Every summer the village held a Lifeboat Day – I think in August – when, on a spring tide, bunting would be hung, and stalls laden with cakes, teas, local crafts, and RNLI branded merchandise, would be set up around the harbour. Mousehole Male Voice Choir would perform an open-air concert at the end of the south pier and the *Solomon Browne* itself would take people out for a trip around St Clement's Isle. The crew members were held in high regard by all, as is a lifeboat crew in every community it serves. The eight from Mousehole were pillars of their community and everyone in the area knew each one of them.

The crew of the *Solomon Browne* were posthumously honoured by the Royal National Lifeboat Institution. Coxswain Trevelyan Richards was awarded the gold medal for his courage and refusal to give up on the crew of the stricken *Union Star*. John Blewett and the rest of the crew, however, were awarded the bronze medal. I never understood that. What more can you give than your life, and yet be awarded bronze. The gold medal service plaque can be seen on the lifeboat station today.

All the lifeboat crew members would have been involved in putting up the Christmas lights that lined the harbour and the hillside. They would have started that work, as they had every year since 1963, at the end of September, working weekends and the odd evening to put the lights in place for nothing other than pleasure and pride in their community. Mousehole Christmas harbour lights were then, and remain so, a special attraction throughout the local area. They were damaged in the storm that fateful night and not repaired the following day, as would usually happen, because of the grief.

But after three days of not illuminating the village, Charlie's widow, Mary, asked for the lights to be repaired and turned back on. There was no objection from anyone, and so it was done. Every 19 December, on the anniversary of the disaster, they are turned off at 8 p.m. for an hour, in remembrance. There is a plaque on the wall of The Ship Inn that reads thus:

Charles Greenhaugh
Landlord of this house
and crewman of the *Solomon Browne*
lost with all hands 19th December 1981
Remembered with great affection
'Greater Love Hath No Man'

The public response to the disaster was amazing. We really felt that support in Mousehole. Over £3 million was raised for the village (which is about £10 million in today's money). That, of course, was a considerable sum of money and quite a showing of support. But it did nothing to ease the pain of the families of the eight men who lost their lives in the name of saving others. I think it is stating the obvious to say that the village has never been quite the same since that fateful day in December 1981. There were many raw emotions: many lifeboat crew members felt a degree of guilt because they weren't on the boat that night, while for others, resentment and anger was felt that their loved ones did. In the years that intervened this became problematic for those left behind.

The danger to life for those who make their living on the sea, especially a lifeboat crew, was brutally evident that night, and it's another episode that underlines how fragile life itself can be. At every turn we are at the mercy of small, seemingly insignificant acts of fate. Both sides of that coin

43

were shown on that December evening. One other volunteer, Neil Brockman, son of crewman Nigel, turned up for duty, but was turned back by coxswain Trevelyan. It was reported that he told Neil that he didn't want two members of the same family on such a mission. Neil's life was saved by that decision. What incredible leadership. Neil has since been the coxswain of that lifeboat service himself; his experience of losing his father when he was just 17 hasn't deterred him in any way – what incredible courage. The *Union Star* captain made an unscheduled stop along the south-eastern coast of England to pick up his wife and two stepdaughters so that they could go on a trip with him. That decision cost the three women their lives.

I didn't know any of that when I was 13, of course. Then, it was just a case of experiencing the most horrible heavy feeling, for the village, and for my friend's family. I didn't understand exactly what had happened that night. I cannot pretend to offer some unique insight now. I can say, however, that I will never forget seeing John Blewett walk out of the door, or the size of the waves and the howls of the gale as we walked home. Nor will I forget the look on my friend's face when I went see him the next morning. I think I realised that his father would never walk back through that same door which I'd watched him leave the night before, but I didn't understand the impact it would have on Andrew. How could I possibly, only Andrew can tell you what that was like.

5

MOUSEHOLE, HOWEVER, WASN'T perfect – it had a football club but it didn't have a rugby club! So the enlightened of the village: myself, Andrew Blewett and Steve Cary, had to pursue our dreams in Penzance. Andrew was a fantastic rugby player, a very skilful outside-half or centre, who was smashing the 'holy bejaysus' out of people as a number 10 about 20 years before Jonny Wilkinson made it mandatory. Steve Cary, or 'Wiggy' as he is affectionately known, was less natural. The good thing was that nobody had told him, or if they had, he'd ignored them. He was your original 100 per center. He left nothing out on the field; he was an outstanding tackler, and despite his lack of any other obvious talent, he went on to become a dual international in cricket and rugby – albeit for Gibraltar – his adopted home. That is more than I or most of the other boys from Mousehole can boast! We played rugby there all year round, mostly on the beach, often in the dark.

Penzance isn't far at all from Mousehole, it's just around the corner. It's not a big town, but big enough to have a nightclub and big enough to have a decent rugby club. Even before they became the 'Cornish Pirates', they had a fabulous set-up there. (It's still one of my favourite grounds.) It had a very big grandstand that ran from roughly one 22-metre line to the other 22-metre line, and held 500 people at capacity. The greatest thing about it, though, was that it had a tunnel which came out from under the stand. It was so narrow, you entered it in single file and ran out onto a beautiful, flat pitch that was enclosed by terrace all the way round the perimeter; it really felt like a stadium and I loved playing there. And so did plenty of others. In the days of Easter club tours, Penzance would be on that circuit. I watched and played against clubs such as Ebbw Vale, Cardiff, Swansea, Wasps, Bristol – they all at one time or another made the trip west to play against Penzance & Newlyn.

I started playing rugby for the Pirates when I was about eight or nine. As in all clubs where mini rugby is played, we were blessed with guys who volunteered to teach us the basics at that young age. Phil Harvey was one. He was a little bit deaf, and we teased him relentlessly, as kids do, only for me to find out as I got to know him better that he was such a lovely guy. Local electrician, Stan Richards, was involved too. They used to play a little rugby themselves and were willing to give their time to teach us. I progressed to playing every age-grade rugby for the Pirates. The under-16s were coached by the father of one of the boys, Steve Berryman. His dad, Dave, has sadly passed away, but he was a monster of a man with a massive smile. He always called me 'Welshman' and I loved him all the more for it. Dave was great player himself and played for Cornwall, but his son Steve went one better and played not only for Cornwall but for the Combined Services against the All Blacks in 1993.

You might recall from the Humphry Davy team sheet earlier that I was a scrum-half at this stage. That might surprise a few people! I was really quite small as a kid, especially at eight years old. Scrum-half was my first position on the rugby pitch, but it wouldn't be my last. I played for the Colts team (the youth team), for four years. It's unusual to play for a youth team for so many years. I started playing for the Colts while I was still at comprehensive school. I carried on playing for the school as well, after becoming a Colt. That meant that I'd play for the school team on Saturday mornings and then play for the Colts in the afternoon. But I was also playing for the under-16s team. So I had to play for them on Sunday! I just couldn't get enough rugby. When it came to weekends as a teenager then, it was all rugby! I often think about boys who are the same age today as I was in those busy rugby days. They are probably playing for regional rugby academies now and, as a result, they're not allowed to play for their village rugby teams. I think that is so wrong. There's no guarantee that you'll get anywhere with an academy. All you want to do as a kid is play, so why not let them just play?

During my 99th game for the Colts, against Hayle, I broke my leg. I was captain that season. I can't really remember much about this, but it would have been at the end of February or the beginning of March. I had to be in plaster for six weeks. My plaster came off on the Friday night before the last game of the end-of-season tour time, and we were due to play Pencoed RFC Youth.

Playing Pencoed was one of our regular fixtures. I'd played against them every season as a Colt. My first ever proper rugby tour was to Bridgend to play Pencoed when I was 16 years old. We stayed at the Esplanade in Porthcawl and we played their youth team on the Saturday and Pencoed on Easter Monday. And we beat them both! That was seen as quite an achievement for us, the team from Cornwall beating a team from that great rugby nation of Wales. It did us a world of good as far as morale was concerned and our coach Colin 'Knocker' Kneebone was well chuffed! But I will never forget our team manger, Ray Jeffery; he was so happy, he had tears in his eyes and gave us all a great bear hug.

I begged to be allowed to start the game so that I could claim those 100 appearances. I think that at the time only one other person, an old team-mate, Peter Small, had played

100 times for the Colts. I wanted to be up there with him. Imagine my excitement when I was allowed to start the game! The boys from Pencoed happily agreed to let me lead my team out for the last time, take up position on the wing, and then leave the field the first time the ball went out of play.

I was happy with that, right up until their outside-half 'shaped' to kick to the forwards and then did a 'funny' by kicking the ball in my direction on the opposite side of the pitch! Remember, the plaster had only just been removed from my leg the day before. My leg was like jelly. I couldn't run or tackle – many would say that was par – but it was especially so that day.

Needless to say, the ball bounced in front of me and over my head; it was gathered by their winger who went past me as if I wasn't there and Pencoed had scored a try within ten seconds. The first break in play was them kicking the conversion! I walked back gingerly to the changing room and watched the rest of the game from the stand. Pencoed beat us that day, with a certain Scott Gibbs playing for them. (I take some comfort from that.) I was so proud to be captain of that team. We only lost twice that year, more materially in the Cup against Redruth. It wasn't bad at all for us to only lose twice in a season. We even beat Wasps Colts the week before the Pencoed game, which I obviously didn't play because I was in plaster. Simon 'Dicky' Stone took my place and played like Gareth Edwards, the b******d. But I was still captain, and I did make my 100th appearance after all – the exact nature of my contribution to that 100th game needn't spoil that fact!

Like my school team, for whom many of the Pirates played, we were pretty successful. We had some cracking players, Berryman, Blewett and 'Wiggy' I've mentioned.

There were others too, too many to mention, who played for Cornwall; some like Simon Stone even went on to play for Bath. We stayed together as a group of lads through this age-grade system, largely because if you live in Penzance there isn't really anywhere else to go apart from St Ives, and that would simply be ridiculous!

As we progressed through the ranks, the senior Pirates team went through a particularly difficult period. Senior rugby clubs are located along the spine of Cornwall, starting at Launceston in the east and ending at Penzance & Newlyn in the west. The Pirates were strong throughout the 1960s and 1970s, with players such as Jimmy Glover, Alvin Williams, Roger Pascoe, Brian Monkton, Mickey James, Stack Stevens, Colin Dymond and any number of Walshes! Throughout the 1980s the Pirates struggled a bit and were regularly hammered by Camborne, Redruth, St Ives and the like; all being very good teams in those days. I must pay grudging respect to that St Ives side. They had some fantastic players: the Corin brothers (especially Roger), Peter Hendy and Louis Stevens (an incredible prop who once chuckled to his front-row colleagues, 'Oooh, we've got a live one here, boys,' when I nutted him on engagement in my first derby game as a tight-head. He subsequently gave me an interesting anatomy lesson that I shall never forget!).

I don't think we've had a proper, full picture of what rugby was like in Cornwall, and it's easy to underestimate both how big the rugby scene was there and how high the standard was. It certainly isn't the backwater people might assume it is because it's so far away, and we don't hear much about what happens on rugby pitches there. It's also easy to dispense platitudes, but all of the players I've mentioned were fine players, many capped at just below full international or had represented the Barbarians. But they lived and worked in Cornwall and so were somewhat off the radar.

That said, Cornwall has produced many international rugby players. The county championship in England was always a production line for international honours until, I guess, around the 1970s and 1980s. By the time the formal Courage National League was introduced, the big clubs, Leicester, Northampton, Wasps etc. had seen the county game fall away in its significance and so they'd no longer release their players for it. There were big West Country clubs too, Gloucester, Bath and Bristol, but they were still a long way from Cornwall.

Players who are driven, however, can still make it. In the last 20 years or so consider these names who have originated from the Grand Duchy: rugged forwards Phil Vickery, Trevor Woodman, Graham Dawe, Martin Haag, Andy Reed, the Vyvyan brothers, Joe Bearman, while Richard Nancekivell, Olly Barkley, Tom Voyce, Colin Laity, and currently Jack Nowell and Luke Cowan-Dickie, two Newlyn boys, show that it's not all grunt in the west.

I honestly believe that Wales and Cornwall have very similar rugby landscapes. Camborne and Redruth are very much like Neath and Aberavon; it's hard to know where one ends and the other one begins, and they hate each other! Another similarity is the fact that these Cornish communities were very much mining ones. Tin miners established them and kept them going until the tin industry declined. The Cornish had been mining for years before the Welsh began to get their hands dirty. Lots of men left Cornwall for Wales to help establish the coal mines that were growing like mushrooms there the nineteenth century. If mining underground wasn't the bread-winning occupation in Cornwall, again, as in south Wales, it would be fishing or farming. And culturally and linguistically, of course, there are longer and stronger Celtic links. There are also religious links – with very many Methodist chapels to be found in both areas. Every village also has its own male voice choir. So I was always very much aware of the strong similarities between Wales and Cornwall, even though I had at the time spent more time in south-west England than in south Wales. Rugby was just another one of those important community activities that both places had in common. There is one other thing that links Cornwall and Wales too, which just cannot be denied. In both places, the further west you go there's less and less chance of any of the bastards buying you a pint!

Cornwall is a long, narrow strip of land with a road going down the middle of it. Every town along that road has a rugby team, just as along the M4 corridor in Wales. The top rugby teams are within a few miles of each other, and there's more than one team in many of the main towns, again much like Wales. This leads to a strong rugby scene, with many intense and fiercely competitive local derbies. These occasions are an integral part of Cornish life.

Outside family life, one of the best days of my life was one occasion when the Pirates played St Ives. Traditionally, that fixture was always a hammering for the Pirates, and being on the end of a 50-point drubbing was quite common for the Penzance boys. We always played against each other sometime between Christmas and the New Year, depending on which leagues the teams were in. It wasn't a Boxing Day fixture, which was also a big rugby tradition in Cornwall. Camborne would play Redruth, and St Ives would play Hayle on that day. Penzance used to play Newlyn, but that no longer happened after the two teams' merger after the Second World War.

The Pirates would play Truro on Boxing Day, which was a right pain as it was about 40 miles up the road and someone had to drive! But, as I've said, we would also play St Ives between Christmas and New Year. I think it was around 1994, after years of 'feedings' down there at the hands of 'The Hakes' (St Ives), that we finally did 'em. Steve Berryman scored the winning try off the back of a scrum with about five minutes to go. By this time my scrum-half days were far behind me. I remember holding out desperately on the tight-head – they had a good pack – and seeing 'Bez' burst past out of the corner of my eye.

What a feeling it was to beat them, and on their own patch. Having been thrashed so many times, a certain resentment had grown amongst us Penzance boys towards St Ives. So the elation at beating them was in direct proportion to the pride and passion we felt after that victory. We had a good few beers all the way back from St Ives, and then back in Penzance itself. A day, a night and an early morning in The Alex to remember... almost! More of The Alex to come.

But strengths can be weaknesses too. Just as in Wales, that type of parochialism – that pride in your own team – can make life difficult in times of change. When the professional era of rugby arrived, businessman Dicky Evans had a vision of bringing top-flight rugby to Cornwall, transforming Penzance & Newlyn into the Cornish Pirates. However, it proved very difficult to develop that critical mass of support throughout the county. It was tough to convince a Camborne season ticket holder to cheer for a team called the Pirates, even if they did play on Camborne's pitch. Perhaps, on a smaller scale, this reflects the simple facts of human nature. Just as people in Wales argue that regions, such as the Ospreys, are a construct, and lack that emotional investment that you get having supported a team 'man and boy'.

When it came to following rugby on television, it was a completely different world to the one I'm now involved with in broadcasting for the BBC. When I was a teenager – which was only in the 1980s – there would only be about a dozen live rugby games a year on the telly. There would be the Five Nations games, and the touring side matches in the autumn, be they the All Blacks or Wallabies. The Five Nations matches weren't staggered either, so they all kicked-off at the same time. You'd have to watch the one the BBC chose to televise live which, rather annoyingly for a Welshman in Cornwall, was England! Other games would be shown later, in highlight form. *Rugby Special* would be on Sundays, with highlights of all the games. I also subscribed to *Rugby World* magazine, which I would read avidly.

On the club rugby front, I followed the fortunes of Newbridge and Cardiff, two teams which dad had played for. The link with Wales was always strong, with rugby being a central component in that chain. I was born in Wales, and it was only natural for me to always keep looking over my shoulder at the land of my fathers. Mum would often take me back to Newbridge to visit the Padfields, with Uncle Chris, Auntie Avril, Ellie and Davey, being the closest thing to family that I have. Whenever dad came back from Australia, we would obviously decamp to Wales.

I had great times further afield, too. I would spend about six weeks every other summer in Australia visiting dad. They play a bit of rugby there too, you know! I managed to squeak into a few teams during my various visits. I played for Clovelly in 1976, for South Coogee in 1979, and for Wentworthville in 1982 and possibly 1984.

By 1984 my dad had remarried and Marlene Matthews became my 'wicked' stepmother! Marlene was an Olympic medallist, winning bronze at the Melbourne Olympics of

1956, and the gold medal at Cardiff's 1958 Empire Games for the 100- and 200-yard race, respectively. Marlene has always been so very kind to me, as have my stepbrothers Craig and Paul, and I must say that as stepmothers go, I could have done a lot worse. Marlene is a highly-respected former athlete in Australia, and that had a lot of fringe benefits. Marlene herself is extremely modest and does not like to take advantage of her standing. I, on the other hand, had no such reservations as a teenager! She is a trustee of the Sydney Cricket Ground; there's even a bar named after her there! As a result, we could go to anything that happened at the SCG, be it cricket (of course), Aussie rules football or international rugby union and league. And I would be sat in the trustees' box, of course. I remember sitting there once and asking who the 'little man over there' was. 'Oh,' came the reply, 'that's Don Bradman'!

I only played a handful of games during those Australian summers, but it was certainly a worthwhile experience.

I watched a lot of rugby out there as well. When dad lived in a block of flats in the Eastern Suburbs, in what he would affectionately call the 'Coogee Hilton', he was about 200 metres from Randwick RFC. I'd walk down to the Coogee Oval every other Saturday morning. This was an amazing pitch, about 100 metres from the beach. Like many in Australia, it also doubled as a cricket pitch. When rugby matches were played there, they would literally place a 300- to 400-metre curtain around the pitch to ensure that if you wanted to see the game you had to pay the few bucks required. You'll understand why in a minute.

The fourth grade team would kick off at 10.30, and I would take my place in the stands to watch that game. Jeff Sayle, at this stage, had become one of my dad's best mates. He played for Australia once, as a flanker, and he was the steward of Randwick Rugby Club and was treated like a god by all involved there. Jeff was still playing in his late 30s, albeit for the fourth grade and as a prop. Just being seen with him meant that I too was treated like a VIP!

I'd then watch the third grade game at midday, the second grade at 1.30 and the first grade at 3 p.m., at which point the curtain would be drawn around the pitch. The reason being? Randwick was the best team in Australia in those days. I was mesmerised by the Ellas: Glen, Gary, and, of course, Mark. By the time I watched them play in the mid-to-late 1980s, these guys had given way to the likes of Ewen McKenzie, Phil Kearns, Simon Poidevin, Lloyd Walker, and a certain unassuming character who played at full-back, but mostly on the wing, called David Campese. Not bad, eh!

6

DAD CAME BACK to Wales for the centenary celebrations of the Welsh Rugby Union in 1981.

My absolute rugby hero was Gareth Edwards. I knew he'd played in the same team as dad and I obviously knew the great heights he'd scaled with Wales and the Lions. I went with dad to Cardiff Rugby Club on the day Cardiff played the All Blacks as part of the centenary celebrations. He was welcomed back like the prodigal son. Gareth Edwards was there, too. He came over to dad and greeted him by his nickname, 'Hey, Tess, how are you?' Dad was called Tess after the Cardiff-born singer and entertainer, Tessie O'Shea. She too was of Irish ancestry, like dad's family. She appeared on *The Ed Sullivan Show* in the United States with the Beatles in 1964 and, on the other end of the scale, Noël Coward wrote a character just for her in one of his shows. I think that sharing the same surname, O'Shea, was an obvious reason why dad got stuck with the nickname Tess. Or was it because Tessie O'Shea adopted the song 'Two Ton Tessie from Tennessee', as her theme tune?

After Gareth Edwards had greeted dad the way he did, dad introduced me to him. I was overwhelmed – it beat seeing Don Bradman hands down. I had an autograph book with me and Gareth agreed to sign it. He put, 'To Richard bach, glad you're not a donkey like your father!' I was still a scrum-half then!

The following Wednesday, the All Blacks were to play Newport. It was a filthy wet, horrible day. I went with dad to that game too, and stood on the terraces with him. I remember the stick he got from his old pals, seeing a Cardiff man on Newport's terraces! After the game, which the All Blacks won, dad went to the clubhouse. There were squash courts inside the club building in those days, and I sat on the steps of the squash courts with can of pop and a bag of crisps. I was waiting for mum to come and pick me up, as dad wanted to enjoy the Newport hospitality a little longer. The squash courts' door suddenly opened, and a figure in a mack and umbrella walked in. He turned round to shake the umbrella and I realised that it was Gareth Edwards. I was amazed. He did a double take and stopped shaking the umbrella. 'Ah, Richard bach!' he said to me, 'Is your dad here?' I just couldn't find any words to answer his question. I lifted my arm and pointed my index finger in the general direction of the bar where dad would have been. I really was dumbstruck. Gareth Edwards not only remembered my name but he spoke to me as well! He then tousled my hair as he walked past me up to the bar. I still feel like that whenever I see him now!

When I was 16 I had another similar experience. I was with dad in Randwick, and the All Blacks were in town. They had either played Australia or Randwick – I can't remember which – but they were there and at the club. Dad introduced me to someone, saying, 'This is Waka Nathan.' That man is a legend of the game, just as Gareth is. He played for the All Blacks from 1962 to 1967, and giants of rugby such as Delme Thomas say that Waka was one of the best ever.

In 1991, a group of dad's mates flew me out to Australia so that I could be a surprise guest at his 50th birthday celebrations. I couldn't quite make it for the actual party as I was in college by then, and exams spoiled the plans. But I flew out a few days later. Dad had been invited by the New Zealand Barbarians to speak at a big luncheon on the eve the

Bledisloe Cup match between Australia and New Zealand at Eden Park in Auckland. He'd been given two business class plane tickets to get him there. Marlene suggested that, as she'd been to Auckland before, why didn't I go with my dad? Five days away on a rugby trip with dad was too good to be true. Dad spoke at the lunch and I sat at the table taking it all in, thoroughly enjoying myself. I went to the toilet, stood at the urinal, and in walked Waka Nathan. He turned to me and asked, 'Is that you, Richard?' I was, once again, dumbstruck. It's always awkward when you meet people in the toilet anyway, but I didn't know how to react to being greeted by the great Waka Nathan while standing at a urinal! Maybe dad's presence at the function had put me in his mind, but it still didn't mean that he would recognise who I was or remember my name. There's a lot in the saying that those who are real greats in their field have so much time for other people. Two rugby legends proved that to me in two different hemispheres. That says a lot about rugby, too.

Back home in Cornwall with mum and nan, life might have seemed a little less glitzy but now, with hindsight, I realise that life was simply fantastic. I'd settle back into the lovely simple life that was ours in Mousehole. As the manageress of the Regent Hotel, mum worked long and hard to ensure that I could keep pace with the other children at St Erbyn's. Because of the kind of hours you have to work in such places, mum wasn't always able to get me ready for or pick me up from school. That's where nan stepped in. She would do all that if mum was working. Nan played a massive part in my life. School holidays were obviously very long, especially in summer, when I was very young. Nan would often take me and our dog, Captain, off in her car – an old convertible Triumph Herald – for day trips. We would have picnics, and fish in the rock pools of all the beautiful beaches and coves that Cornwall has in abundance. Sundays were special in those days; mum would return home from the hotel and we'd all have Sunday lunch together. In the late 1970s my nan's sister, Auntie Glad, was widowed, and she joined us in Mousehole. So there we all were, a little Welsh enclave. I was spoiled rotten by these three Welsh ladies and I exploited them mercilessly! They all made sure that, within reason, I wanted for nothing. Nan and Auntie Glad have passed away and I hope they knew how much I loved them and how grateful I was.

So, in Cornwall, it was not a case of having top-of-the-range sporting facilities, but just making the best of what we had and enjoying life. I've already mentioned the Christmas lights in the harbour, and the fact that work would start to get the quays ready months in advance. This often meant that the handrails along the harbour wall and the upright posts holding the layers of lanterns would be in place, but unfinished, for a long time. They were ideal rugby posts.

They didn't make replica shirts in those days, like they do now, but I had a red shirt which had the three feathers on it. I would proudly put this shirt on and run down to the harbour where I would play for Wales – on my own. I easily won about a thousand caps for Wales during that period! I can't tell you how many international tries I scored – and it wasn't John Taylor who kicked that winning conversion for Wales against Scotland, it was me! And no one ever asks my opinion on any rugby world issues, as an ex-international of such standing!

The row of cottages that included our home gave me early cricket experience, too. There were three cottages in a row and a path nearby leading up to other cottages at a dead end. There was no shortage of walls, therefore. I would spend hours throwing a tennis ball at one of these walls, a bat in my other hand, ready to knock the ball for six as soon as it came back to me off the wall. During those times I was Ian Botham.

I played football for a while until I realised, years after everybody else, that I was crap at it. I loved skiing too, and thanks to the trinity of ladies I've just mentioned, I went on regular skiing holidays. I loved sailing, and I got involved with the Penzance Sailing Club. I loved taking my little Laser dinghy out on the sea. If I showed any interest in any of these sports or activities, my mum would encourage me as much as she could, and do all that she could to help me develop them further. I like to think that I appreciated it, that I actually wasn't a spoilt little brat. I felt at the time that I was being loved and given the best upbringing I could possibly have. I certainly appreciate it now. I probably don't thank her often enough either, but quite simply, without her, I wouldn't have been able to do all the things that someone thought would make a good read.

But all that said, I suppose it's possible to analyse it all now and say that it was a double-edged sword. I did all these lovely things, but I didn't have to put any effort into it, it all just happened for me. I didn't pay my school fees, I didn't pay to go on skiing holidays – it was all done for me. All the other wonderful things I experienced came to me – I didn't have to go to get them. Perhaps this meant that I had difficulties in later adult life, as I had a hell of a job adjusting to things that weren't laid on a plate for me.

I had always worked, though. It's not as if I was always on the take, that's not what I'm saying. Because of where we lived, summer and Christmas jobs were easy to come by, such as helping to deliver mail in the morning and then working for a local building firm the rest of the day. At another time

I delivered bottled gas for the J. H. Bennett gas firm. And of course, I worked behind the bar at the Coastguard pub, and washed the dishes in the Cornish Range. I also worked when in I was visiting Australia.

My work ethic was OK and always has been. But just as I found school life difficult at Humphry Davy after year three – because St Erbyn's had given me a head start in my education up until that point – so fighting for my place in a rugby team proved to be challenge when I left Cornwall.

That time came when I finished the sixth form, and college life beckoned. It was almost inevitable that I had to leave Cornwall for that to happen. Village life was fantastic, a sense of community was there, the almost idyllic times which will always be close to my heart. I still had my warm childhood memories, and they were very strong positive ones. But the next big step in my life was right in front of me, and I knew I had to leave all that behind. As I look back now at the time of my standing at that crossroads, the words of Mike Jenkin, the head at St Erbyn's, come back to me. In my final school report he wrote those words that have been relevant in many different ways throughout my life: 'Richard has the "big match" potential, but will he be selected?'

I was given every opportunity in life. But it has always haunted me that I didn't make the most of it. There were times when I could have been selected, but I wasn't. I don't think I can say that I took my rightful place on the pitch for the big match until I started to study medicine a few years ago. But that's for later. The next step took me back to Wales.

7

WHEN I WAS 18, all I wanted to do was play rugby and drink beer, and that's pretty much what I did. I got to the end of sixth-form college, but how I will never know. On the way there, I stuffed up my O Levels spectacularly. That was 1984, the summer I was going to see dad in Australia. So not concentrating fully on my exams was quite easy. As previously mentioned, I was entered for ten O Levels. But I didn't do any work on most subjects, especially the sciences that needed a bit of hard graft to get to grips with them. I didn't actually get to sit Chemistry; Physics was a nightmare subject for me, as was Maths, but I was always quite good at Biology. To be honest, I can't remember which subjects I actually took in the end. What is quite clear in my mind though, is that, as mentioned, I failed all of them apart from two, History and Geography. Such failure really gave me the impetus I needed to be better, and I worked really hard at the resits. I went to sixth-form college, but I used the first year there to resit my O Levels. I did well and passed them all. I could then move on to A Levels, but a year behind all my friends who were by then starting their second year at A Level.

Sixth-form college was just like any typical scene from American high school movies! We all thought we were so cool, with our hooded training tops and our jeans and trainers. I stood around the radiator that the first XV rugby boys hung around, often wearing the green county rugby jumper which was a veritable badge of honour which separated you from the rest. I had hair in those days, a rather ridiculous blond mop, with a bit of a mullet. It was sort of halfway between a George Michael bouffant and a Spandau Ballet flick. I thought I looked good – I was in a minority of one!

I chose Geography and Social Biology for A Level. I didn't think I had it in me to sit three A Levels. My P.E. teacher, John Matthews, took me through my Human Biology resit and thought that Social Biology would suit me. He was another one of those people I looked up to. His wife, Christine, was a great friend of my mum's, and he was also a keen sailor who I'd come across at the sailing club. He encouraged me in school, which was a big help. I never really thought that studying was important. I'd developed an interest in girls but, broadly speaking, I was far more interested in where my next pint came from than when my next date would be. If I was on a date, I would always think that I was missing out on some fun with the rugby boys somewhere else. So school work was incidental to actually enjoying life.

At the end of my time at school I was chosen to be part of something quite special. Along with two other boys from the school, Richard Brownfield and that bloody Hake, Billy Peters, I was chosen to go to Bisham Abbey for a one-week rugby residential summer school run by the RFU. Those chosen to go were seen as potential England Schoolboy U16 (under 16) internationals, and we were selected from all over the country. We were split into four squads and the week's training sessions built up to a tournament at the end when the four squads would play against each other. There must have been boys there who went on to play rugby for England, but the only one I can remember was Roger Twose, a Devon boy who also went on to play cricket for New Zealand. In the county game, playing for Warwickshire, Twose was one of Brian Lara's partners when he scored his massive 501 not out against Durham in 1994.

Ironically, I wasn't even good enough to get into the Cornwall under-16s team the following season, let alone England. My way was barred by an outstanding 15 year old from St Agnes, Howard Davy. I was utterly devastated; not only was he a superb player, he was also incredibly handsome and I think his dad owned a brewery! I thought that I was lucky!

Eventually, at under-18 level, I was chosen to play for Cornwall. My first game was against the Royal Air Force, a game I remember much more for the bus breaking down on the way there and then us getting lost and being unable to find the RAF camp in north Somerset! The post-match photo is to be remembered for my ridiculous hairstyle – well it was the 1980s. In it I'm proudly wearing the famous black and gold of Cornwall, with my hair the same colour as the gold hoops on my shirt. My mate's mum was a hairdresser and she offered to dye it for me, possibly because I erroneously believed that it was because of Howard Davy's blond hair that the selectors preferred him to me! Sadly, the experiment failed, and instead of beach-boy blonde it turned out to be some kind of carroty, coppery, goldish shade of turd.

I played in a few more warm-up games before the county championships started properly. These were regarded as the trials to see if you could get into the England Schoolboys' squad. For us in Cornwall, the championship meant games against Devon, Somerset and Gloucestershire. Historically, Gloucestershire was the foremost rugby county in the south west, with a long tradition of the sport. Bristol would have been regarded as being in Gloucestershire for years, and that would have strengthened the county's rugby pedigree considerably. Cornwall probably would come second to Gloucestershire, ahead of Somerset and Devon.

I was chosen for the first championship game against

Somerset in Taunton. Not only did I keep out 'pretty boy' Davy, but I also relegated Simon Enoch, my long-time rival and fellow Welsh boy living in Cornwall, who was also a scrum-half. Simon was also a cracking player, by *also* I mean also like Howard Davy… not me! Simon eventually worked his way back home and played for Pontypridd and we remain good mates.

We narrowly lost to Somerset in Taunton. I don't recall much else from that game, except the immortal line from our coach, Floyd Barnett, delivered at half-time and directed to our full-back, a fellow Pirate, Damon Horrocks:

'Damon, try not to let the ball bounce in front of you.'

'Why not?' came a truculent reply.

'Because it makes you look like a c***.'

The following week, in early December, we were to play Gloucestershire in Newquay. These were the worst possible conditions for a game of rugby. The pitch itself was on a headland and the weather was atrocious. What a combination. We won, 4–0. Another old pal, Martin Haag, who won his Schoolboys' cap that year, before winning a full cap out of Bath, scored the only points of the game. He caught the ball in a line-out and we drove him over the line. There was no way the conversion would have gone over even if he'd fallen under the posts. That's about as exciting as it got. Actually, now I think of it, his second-row colleague for Cornwall that day was Andy Reed, who went on to play for Scotland and the Lions – nobody was surprised that 'Haagy' went all the way, but none of us saw that coming!

Andy Reed was born in St Austell and played for Bodmin RFC, but he decided that he was Scottish and played for their national team when they were pretty handy! But, more than that, he was also chosen for the British and Irish Lions, too. He played against the All Blacks in 1993. Legend has it that Andy, Mike Teague and Scott Gibbs were in the toilet of an Auckland bar after the third and final Test at Eden Park. The bloke standing next to the three, a fan who had travelled out to follow the Lions, looked up and realised who he was having a pee next to. He apologised for not being able to shake hands with the boys, due to their current circumstances, but he continued to praise them for the game they'd just played and waxed lyrical about their virtues and strengths. That is, he praised two of the three; he wasn't so fulsome in his thoughts of Andy's performance and started to say things like, 'don't think he had his best game'. Andy took exception to the comments and started ranting that he'd had enough of fans commenting, criticising and the like, and then he upped the ante considerably by inviting the fan outside so that they could sort it out once and for all. The poor bloke looked shaken and stunned. He was in his 60s if he was a day. As he left the toilet, Mike Teague turned to Scott and whispered – 'My money's on the old guy!' – allegedly. Or it could just be a joke!

At the post-match dinner after we beat Gloucestershire, I sat as proud as a peacock in my white shirt, county tie and bottle green county jumper. My opposite number sat across the table from me. I looked at him and realised that he was an English Schoolboy international, his red tie and silver blazer badge trumping my county colours hands down! His name was Bruce Fenley, and he went on to captain Gloucester in his senior career. I was later chosen as a non travelling reserve for the South and South West team when, under bizarre circumstances, Brett Taylor, the Somerset scrum-half, did an 'Andy Reed' and decided he too was Scottish and was no longer eligible for the England under-18s!

All these new experiences, especially the ones that took

me out of the county, gave me a more realistic picture of where I stood in the grand scheme of things on a rugby pitch. Outside Cornwall I did sometimes feel like a little fish in a big pond. By this time I was getting physically stronger and was playing first-team games for the Pirates. I could pass off both hands; I couldn't kick so well off both feet, but I could kick at goal. And that was good. But I was also becoming a little slower around the pitch. If you're 18, 19, you need to be quick off the mark. It would be very difficult for me to go into senior rugby as a slow scrum-half. It would be OK to be a slow number 9 if you were in your 30s, as you know all the dark arts that can compensate for your lack of speed. But it doesn't work like that if you're 18 or so. And people started to notice. I remember Mike Williams, a P.T. instructor in the Navy and a scrum-half for the Pirates, telling me that I needed to get into the pack, that my lack of speed was starting to show. I just thought he was being a dick, but he was absolutely right and I wish I'd listened to him.

John Matthews also suggested as much to me one day, giving me plenty of food for thought. He told me once, after a bit of a knock-about game between a few of the lads, that if I was ever given an offer to move up north, to rugby league territory, that I should accept the offer without hesitation. Their game, he said, of head down and crack on with it, would suit me fine. But I was too slow to be a rugby union scrum-half. He had a solution, too. He thought I should go into the back row. I parked that idea in the back of my mind, and soldiered on with number 9 on my back. But what kept on coming back to my thoughts was my time at Bisham Abbey. I think I secretly knew then that scrum-half wasn't to be for me. John's comments had fallen on already prepared ground.

I persevered at scrum-half and was chosen to captain Cornwall for a weekend tour to watch an England Five Nations match at Twickers. We were to play Hampshire on the way up to London and then play Middlesex on the way back home. Both of our games were cancelled due to heavy snow. I didn't get my chance to captain my county. The following year I was invited to go on the same tour again, even though I was a year too old. Apparently, they thought that I'd be good value on the trip, even though I couldn't play at 19 years of age.

However, by this time I'd my broken leg. As I tried to stand on the Twickenham terraces, watching England play Scotland, some bloke decided to urinate all over my plaster. He thought it was hysterical. I didn't. As a result of that reckless act, as well as me having to hobble around on it all day, my plaster cracked. On the bus on the return to Cornwall – which was a very posh bus for those days, as it had a toilet in it – I went for a pee myself. Once finished, I came out of the cubicle but someone on the bus had used my crutch to block me in. I was locked in that very small toilet for about an hour until I managed to push hard enough to free myself. But unfortunately, in the process, I snapped my crutch! I arrived home, therefore, on a broken, sodden plaster, with a crutch in two pieces.

Side by side with this rugby activity, there was still the matter of where I would go after sixth-form college. What was I going to do with my life? With Martin Haag I decided to join the police force. There was a feeling that if you were a sportsman in the police force you would do all right. That was enough for me. But it was more than enough for my mother. She wasn't keen at all on the idea. She worried that I'd end up one day having to give a druggie the kiss of life, and that was just too much for her. My response to her protestations was not only insisting that I'd join the police, but adding that I really, really wanted to join the Royal Ulster Constabulary. Her reaction is not printable!

University was not an option. I'd realised that I wasn't cut out for academia. However, one day, I had a phone call from Leighton Davies, a senior lecturer and head rugby coach at South Glamorgan Institute, the former Cyncoed Teacher Training College in Cardiff, an absolute rugby Mecca which has been rebranded a number of times since, recently as UWIC, and is now known as Cardiff Metropolitan University. He was also a pal of my father's, having been at St Luke's at the same time. He also played in the back row for Bridgend and Maesteg. I'm very proud to say that he is now a good friend of mine.

Mr Davies, as we always called him to his face, was a legend at Cyncoed. His nickname, when he wasn't around, was Nutty! Everyone was terrified of him, despite the fact that he was only about four foot two! He was a man who, shall we say, didn't suffer fools gladly. Leighton had been out to Australia to visit his brother. He'd met up with my old man while out there, and dad obviously told him that I wasn't too sure where to go next after sixth-form college. On the phone Leighton asked me if I'd thought about going to a P.E. college. I told him that it hadn't crossed my mind at all. I was also fairly convinced, I said, that I'd never get the grades needed to get into such a college. He had an answer though. 'You might be able to get in on a HND Business and Finance course at the Colchester Avenue campus. How would you feel about that?' I immediately asked if that meant I could still play rugby. He said that if I was good enough I could certainly play for a college XV. He'd planted the seed that even if I didn't get high enough grades to go straight onto a degree course, there might be other things I could do instead. He made me think that there was no need to dismiss academia entirely, especially as it meant I could go on playing rugby... a lot!

In what would become a typical twist of good fortune in my life, the director of the HND course was a chap called John Luke, and he was the brother of a lovely lady, Rachel Hood. Rachel and I worked in the same restaurant, the Cornish Range in Mousehole. I'd end up becoming great friends with his son, also John, and share a house with him when we became reps together in Cornwall.

So that was it. The day came when mum drove me to south Wales, not for our usual family and friends visit this time, but so that I could begin my Business and Finance studies at the South Glamorgan Institute of Higher Education, the college of knowledge on the hill.

8

I'LL NEVER FORGET watching my mum drive away from the Cyncoed campus. I sat in my room, on my bed, with my bag nearby, looking through the window as she left. Any camaraderie, community spirit, and closeness that had been in my life for the best part of 18 years seemed to be so far, far away. I remember thinking to myself, it's sad here, what am I going to do? I sat there in this state for a while, and then there was a knock at the door. It opened and a head popped round it, a shorn head with a smile showing a metal peg where a crowned tooth should have been, the crown having long gone. He looked very much like Jimmy Nail, but it wasn't him. It was Marc Hughes. By pure coincidence, it turned out that he was the son of Arthur Hughes, who'd played for Newbridge with my father, and Marc was also the nephew of Dennis Hughes who was capped for Wales. Dennis was at Lewis School, Pengam, with my dad. Marc said, 'A' right, butt?' And that was it. I never looked back. The two of us went out for a drink or two, and then straight into the non-stop freshers' fortnight. College life was now well and truly mine!

We both played in the freshers' rugby trial and got into the first XV squad along with another fresher, Richard Boladz, a very talented full-back from Ystradgynlais. I think we might have been the only freshers to get into the first XV squad for the first game of the season. I can't remember who we played or what the result was. But I can remember the 'Buzz Circle'. This was a generic name given to playing a variety of increasingly ridiculous games to expedite the process of becoming sauced up!

It was a tradition to hold a Buzz Circle after each game. The entire team would sit in a circle wearing our number ones – the full uniform: shirt, tie, blazer. The captain was, more often than not, the chairman holding supreme power over the cohort in the circle. We would play all sorts of stupid drinking games with all sorts of stupid rules: rules such as, no showing of teeth, left handed drinking, pointing with elbows only. We were not allowed to address the chairman directly, only through another member of the team, and so on. One of our number would be the 'Clec', the one charged with policing the circle and telling tales about any breach of the aforementioned rules, or any perceived errors in the execution of games (which included making a lot up as well, just for the sheer hell of it!). It was great fun!

While they were clearly the types of events that were the very epitome of the 'rugger bugger' stereotype, these rituals became the stuff of absolute legend and were a rite of passage, too. People would gather around just to watch us play these games, or possibly just to observe it as a social experiment in much the same way as you'd laugh at a chimps' tea party.

Today, such a thing would be utterly frowned upon, because of its irresponsibility and recklessness. The whole purpose of these games in the Buzz Circle was to make people drink so much that they'd eventually throw up. Freshers had special treatment at their first Buzz Circle, having to take off a left shoe and put it in a bin in the middle of the circle. Yes, of course, you've guessed it. That was the same bin which everyone would run to when they wanted to puke. When that happened – and it was when, not if – everybody else would jump to their feet, raise their arms in the air and sing 'Fry's Turkish Delight' in keeping with the tune for the said product on the TV advert. This could go on for a while, because as the game progressed, more and more of us would rush to that bin and we could be repeating our chant for ages. I have no idea why we sang that song!

The chairman of my very first Buzz Circle was a fellow by the name of Dai Rees. He went on to play outside-half for Newbridge and Newport, as well as being capped for Wales B. He's now the top man in Hong Kong Rugby. At that time, just as now, he was a good-looking guy. He had a moustache like Graham Gooch and looked permanently tanned like Nigel Davies, the centre. We called him 'Deckchair Dai', not because of his tan, but because he folded easily under pressure!

At my first Buzz Circle, he asked all the freshers who'd made their debut that day to introduce themselves. Before we did, he said that we'd be given new names which we'd be known by throughout the rest of our days in college. Marc stood up and said his name. Dai spotted the Jimmy Nail-look that Marc had going on, and decided he looked like 'Oz'; so he was given the name 'Oz' (which he's still known by to this day). It was my turn next.

'I'm Richard O'Shea,' I said.

He collapsed laughing before managing to say, 'What? F*****g Rick O'Shea?'

Further laughter followed, from him and the others.

'What a stupid name!' Dai continued, 'I can't believe that!'

Needless to say, I was never known as anything but Rick from that day onwards. In Cornwall, no one ever calls me Rick because I was never known as Rick there. I'm either called Fatty or O'Shea or, very occasionally, just Richard. I wasn't allowed to have my real name – albeit altered as it had just been – as my Buzz Circle name. So Dai came up with another nickname for me. He decided I looked like a former college scrum-half called Nigel Gibson. So my nickname was to be 'Gibson'. I'd had two name changes within five minutes, having had the same one for 19 years! On christening me Gibson, Dai couldn't resist going back to my proper name. 'Can you believe that! Rick O'Shea! Rick O'Shea! General laughter everyone.' So everyone had to obey the chairman and laugh as hard as they could at my name, pointing at me as they did so. Every ten minutes or so, throughout the remainder of that Buzz Circle, Dai would turn and point at me and say my name again and call for more general laughter, which duly followed. And my punishment for being called Rick O'Shea was to down a pint in one.

Later on, future first-class rugby star, Tony Copsey, would be a big part of the Buzz Circles, with his speciality being drinking a pint while standing on his head. But that proved to be insufficient to impress The Circle after a while, and he was told to drink a pint of puke while standing on his head. It really did get that ridiculous. Some would get drunk really quickly, of course, and would be running back and forth to the bin quite a lot. In fact, they would often puke themselves sober again, but they weren't allowed to leave the circle.

For some alcohol presented no challenge. Despite their constant failure to remember to say 'Buzz' on the count of seven or 'Fizz' on the count of five, and the successive requirement to dispatch two or four 'fingers', half of it, or the whole pint, some miscreants would still make the same mistakes. These people would be subject to more imaginative punishments. They might, as we were at a P.E. college, be required to execute a forward roll or something similar; they might be required to walk up to the prettiest girl in the

Union and say, 'Hello, I'm Rick Astley' and then sing two verses of 'Never gonna give you up!' with full choreography.

However, some were utterly useless and defiant, and for them there was an ultimate sanction, a special treatment. They had what we called a ten-second 'Ashworth'. John Ashworth was the New Zealand flanker who had stamped on J.P.R. Williams' head during an infamous tour game against Bridgend. The 'accused' would have to adopt the foetal position on the floor, with the chairman nominating three players to stamp on him. On one occasion, an Ashworth managed to break the nose of one of the boys. He didn't put a complaint in, but the bar staff saw it and the result was the banning of Buzz Circles anywhere on campus. They were probably right to do that, as there was a genuine fear of where the whole thing would end, and how much more stupid it would get.

But it was only banned on campus. The answer then was to move our meetings down to the Claude pub. The students' union bar staff were, of course, gutted. They'd lost all that substantial, regular trade and the Claude was now benefiting. Until that is, the Claude banned us too. So we moved to the Albany pub. The pubs were right to ban us too, because at five o'clock on a Saturday afternoon, as people were having a quiet drink, there would be utter carnage nearby, with puke and beer flowing. But a clever guy – called Rick, spookily enough – took over the Claude and realised the potential in having up to 20 lads in every week. He told us we could have an upstairs room to ourselves. I worked my way up to be chairman of the Buzz Circle myself. Cyncoed was, quite simply, bonkers!

We did have fantastic rugby talent though, it must be said. I've already mentioned Tony Copsey, who went on to play for the Scarlets and Wales and to be chief executive at

Wasps. Stuart Davies, the international number 8 and BBC rugby pundit, was there then as well. Dai Bryant was capped from college. In my second year were Jonathan Humphreys, who would win over 30 caps for Wales as well as captain his country, and Paul John who also won 14 caps for Wales. John Devereux, in time a dual code rugby international and a British Lion, had just left, but his midfield partner, Colin Laity, a regular at Neath and later a Barbarian, stopped on for the postgraduate teaching certificate. Later Matthew Back and Dai Manley arrived, also Alan Carter, an already capped flanker from Newport. And I've already mentioned Dai Rees. There are so many more that really were superb rugby players and would have shone far more had they not been among such illustrious company during their college days. Two of these were Huw Davies and Rhodri Ogwen Williams. I met these two at college and they would play a central role in my life afterwards. More about them, later.

So I was a student. I did the HND with a view to moving on to do a P.E. degree, or as I affectionately like to refer to it, the 'hopping and skipping' course. I settled into college routine very well, with the studies during the week seen as a lead up to the weekend events of rugby matches, Buzz Circle, a visit to the Claude, an Indian curry, and so on. The Indian restaurants of Cardiff got to know us quite well; usually, however, for our misbehaviour, such as doing a runner without paying. There was a time when I was banned from all the Indians restaurants in Roath (of which there were many), not only for doing runners, but for general merriment, such as dancing in the fish pond, attempting leg spin bowling with an onion bhaji, and various other similar activities. Looking back at such behaviour now, I'm sure it's easy for me to think that I was totally over the top and no good at all. But then, it was very much a rite of passage that was definitely of its time. My mullet had gone by then, and I sported the then fashionable *Top Gun*-type flat top, short hairstyle.

During our first year we terrorised campus. I lived in Basset 3. In the second year you could move off campus and into student houses, mostly in Roath and Cathays. I lived in a house on Keppoch Street, Roath, with some boys from the Business Studies course. Marc Hughes (Oz), was one of them. He would spend most of his time in his room listening to Northern Soul. There was also Stephen Painter, a scrum-half from Nelson, and a public school lad from Macclesfield, Julian Jones. I still owe him some money I think, because I borrowed his car to go to get some cash from a machine on Wellfield Road, but was distracted on the way by the form of a female jogger, and went into the back of another car in the process. Julian paid to repair the damage because I wasn't insured to drive his car! I agreed to pay him back £20 a month but, by my reckoning now, I only ever made that first payment. A Welsh-speaking boy from Aberaeron, Mathew Mathias, also shared with us, and he was into heavy metal and classical music. Quite a combination!

Mathew was the one we used to hide in various cupboards around the house when the landlord called round to collect the rent. Most of us somehow managed to keep just enough money back out of the beer and curry account to pay the rent, but Mathew didn't always succeed. We had pine-clad living room walls in that house, and spent a lot of time in that room playing three-card brag, usually a little worse for wear. In such a state, we'd often stand Mathew up against one of the walls and throw knives at him. Being an avid viewer of horror films and a subscriber to *Fangoria*, he took it all in his stride. Tim Neumann was also there, a guy from west Wales, even though he had a German surname. He was into The Smiths and all the Manchester-scene music. We were a mixed bunch but a good bunch. Girlfriends came and went but, as I said before, having a girlfriend or not didn't really bother me then. Some of us in that house, naming no names, were living proof that even the sun shines on a dog's arse now and again!

The rugby was a constant, of course. Oz was a cracking forward and often played in the first team; he'd occasionally get selected for Newbridge and was either a number 8 or second row. My friend Huw, who I mentioned earlier, was either number 8 or blind-side. They were both very similar characters. For 18-year-old boys they were very dogged and mature in rugby terms. If we played teams that weren't student teams – which we often did – men in those teams always wanted to rough us student types up a bit. I remember one game in Abercynon on a Monday night. Perhaps I run the risk of never being welcomed again to Abercynon, but the story is worth telling.

We had an impressive pack that night, which included Huw, Oz, a big loose-head called John Hubbard, Jonathan Humphreys, and big bad Tony Copsey. It was a second-team fixture but Copsey, who by now we'd nicknamed 'Fletch' (because he'd been arrested at his brother's stag do and had spent a night in the cells), was playing for some reason. So too, I think, was Paul John.

The Abercynon boys decided that we were ripe for a hammering. Happily, I was on the bench, and so had the perfect view of what unfolded. It was utter carnage. The highlight was one of the Abercynon boys taking off like Lynn 'the leap' Davies, and landing two-footed on Huw's chest as he lay on his back at the side of the ruck. All hell broke loose. But none of our boys took a single backward step, except possibly Scott 'Ronnie' Corbett who ran 70 yards to finish off the try, only to look around and see the other 29 players involved in a massive brawl somewhere around the halfway line. We were soon winning – both the fights and the game. The few locals who braved the elements that evening didn't like *that* fact, either. I will never forget one heckle from the stand:

'Oh come on, ref, they've only come here for a fight!'

I didn't get to play many times against the Llanellis or Cardiffs, but whenever we did, those clubs didn't need to beat you up – they just simply outplayed you. I remember playing against Tredegar and Penarth, and we gave both those teams a bit of a run, beating Tredegar on one occasion. That was the difference I saw in playing rugby in Wales. When I played against Redruth or Camborne, I was playing against teams which included really good rugby players. But when you played against Pontypridd or Neath, you didn't play against a team who had four or five really good players, you played against a team who had 15 of them. In student rugby it was also quite strange to be playing against a certain team one week, and then the following week seeing that same team playing their next match on telly.

In the autumn of 1987 there were three scrum-halves in the first-team squad: Richard Williams, a Welsh Schoolboys' international who went on to play for Newport and Ebbw Vale; Stuart Jardine, a South African lad who won a cap for Scotland through his ancestry; and then there was me. I had still hung on to my number 9 shirt, despite my growing doubts about my suitability for that position. But I got into the first XV at college, so I couldn't have been that bad.

We did our best to support Wales, as well. In my first year, a trip was organised to see the Triple Crown decider in Dublin. Wales had already beaten England at Twickenham, thanks to Adrian Hadley's two tries. We'd also beaten

Scotland in Edinburgh, thanks to some magic from Jiffy (Jonathan Davies) and sidestepping from Ieuan Evans. So it was off to Dublin to see if we could beat the Irish and clinch the Triple Crown. One of my fellow students, Andy Loughlin, organised the trip and in the end about 40 of us went out there. Half the gang would be playing for Cyncoed in a match in Dublin, and the other half would play a Welsh Colleges' match in Dundalk.

Eight o'clock on the Wednesday morning, and the train pulled out of Cardiff station with us students on board. The train chugged its way through mid Wales to Crewe where we got off and caught the connection to Holyhead. When I got to Holyhead I bought a case of Stella Artois and split it with Phil Haynes, six cans for him, six for me.

When we got off the ferry in Ireland – and this is absolutely true – I saw an old lady carrying a heavy bag down the gangplank, so I stopped to help her. I got her and myself safely to the bottom and saw her on her way. I turned round to go back to join the boys, but they weren't there. I couldn't find them anywhere. I didn't have any money; I didn't think that my card would work in any Irish cash machine, so I was stuck. I found a taxi and explained my situation to the driver. With typical Irish hospitality he said, 'Go on, jump in, we'll sort you out when we get there.' So off we went.

There was an Irishman in college with us, David MacAnally, who we called Dai. I think his dad was the manager of a leisure centre in the suburbs of Dublin, a place called Coolmine. That's where we were all going to stay on our trip, sleeping on the floor of the gym. So the taxi driver drove me to this leisure centre. But, when we got there, there was no sign of the boys. A staff member suggested that the gang might have gone to such and such a pub. The cabby, fair play to him again, said that he would take me there. Luckily, the lads were there, camped in one corner, well settled into drinking their pints. I paid the taxi man having borrowed some cash, and settled down to drink with my fellow students. They, of course, were more than up for giving me a hard time for getting lost and separated from them, teasing and goading me relentlessly.

I was fairly well oiled by that time, of course, but I still needed another drink. I walked up to the bar and asked for a Guinness. The barman turned to me and said, 'So, is your name O'Shea? You with these boys from Cardiff?' He must have heard the boys using my name when they were giving me stick for getting lost. I confirmed that that was my name and that I was with the boys. 'Did your father play for Wales and the Lions in the 1960s?' he asked. Rather taken aback, I said yes. And the barman said, 'Right, you come with me!' and he led me out of the pub, ushered me into his car and drove me to his pal's pub about two miles away.

There was a guy at that pub who'd been on tour with my dad for a representative team (possibly the Irish Wolfhounds). I was introduced to him and he duly sat me in the corner of the bar and proceeded to tell me story after story about dad, while plying me with drink the whole time. They wouldn't let me buy a drink, and afterwards they drove me back to Coolmine Leisure Centre. Just incredible!

The set-up at the leisure centre was that we were to sleep on small crash pads. Sleep didn't come easily to most of us, and we started to muck about. As you can imagine, a lot of these memories are vague, but we had a big prop called Richard Erskine, and I think it was him that we carried (while asleep on his crash pad), out of the gym and to the room next door – the swimming pool! We placed him carefully at the edge of the pool, so that if he rolled over in the night, he would plop into the water. Which, of course, he did!

That first day had been rather eventful, to say the least. The following day those representing Welsh Colleges had their game against Irish Colleges in Dundalk. We all went up there, whether we were playing or not. It went very well. Welsh Colleges were 20–0 up at half-time. Then the effects of the previous day's beer kicked in, and we lost 27–20! In the clubhouse afterwards, the bus driver came up to us and told us that he'd be leaving to take us back to Dublin dead on ten o'clock. This was the late 1980s, and, as Dundalk was on the border with Northern Ireland, he didn't want to hang around there too long into the night. He was true to his word and at exactly ten we were on our way. All of us but two, that is. Both had to catch a train back the next day; I think female distraction was the reason they missed the bus!

The next day, Cyncoed were to play an Old Belvedere XV, a very good first-class Irish side. So someone, in their infinite wisdom, had arranged a game for us on the Friday night before a Five Nations international. As mentioned, I'd been on the pop all day when we travelled from Wales, also the whole of the following day (as I wasn't playing for Welsh Colleges) and, on Friday, someone also had the genius idea of arranging a sightseeing tour of the Guinness Brewery at ten in the morning! When we arrived, the guy who met us at the gate took one look at us, and asked if we wanted to do the tour or just go straight to the bar where there were free samples. That was an absolute no brainer of a question, of course!

We settled quite comfortably in that bar, drinking Guinness from the Guinness goblets they provided. In our party was an American postgraduate student from Long Beach University in Los Angeles. There were a few postgrads with us, seven in total, and they sang 'The Magnificent Seven' song whenever they were together. As well as the

American, there was Dai Rees, Colin Laity, Steffan Phillips and Tony Rees. We'd call Tony 'Shark Attack', not because of the way he played his rugby, but because he looked as if he'd come off worst in a shark attack! To be fair, that might have been his brother... but hey, never let the truth get in the way of a good story! It was the American's 21st birthday, and that gave us another reason to celebrate. The Guinness sampled was so creamy, we could stand 21 matches upright in the froth – a far better birthday cake than a jam sponge!

We came to the end of our time at the Guinness Brewery and headed off to a few more Dublin pubs. Come late afternoon, it was time to travel to Old Belvedere to play our match. We caught the bus – a public transport bus, not a coach all to ourselves – and made our way towards their ground which is near Donnybrook, and towards Dún Laoghaire. 'Nutty,' our coach Leighton Davies, sat at the front of this double-decker bus. But he fell asleep, which is rather ironic, as he'd spent the day sightseeing and hadn't been on the pop with the rest of us (who were still awake, at least). So, when we got to our stop, we all tiptoed past him and got off, leaving him to continue the journey to some other part of Ireland.

Leighton caught up with us eventually and I remember him telling me and my outside-half in the dressing room that evening, 'Richard O'Shea and Michael Groom, I want you to play like international half-backs tonight!'

The game started at a furious pace. In the first 15 minutes it seemed that Nutty's team talk had done the trick. I scored two tries and Groomy converted them! But it wasn't long before I didn't feel very well at all. I just couldn't keep up with the pace of the game. It would have been a challenge had I been completely drink-free but, after three all-day-ers, it was more than a challenge. I had to come off. Nutty was in the clubhouse, which ran along the touchline. He got wind of the fact that I was 'carrying a knock'. He was told that I was coming off, to be replaced by Richard Herborne.

He raced down to the touchline and came up to me, 'Richard O'Shea, what's the matter with you?'

'It's my shoulder Mr Davies, I think I might have popped it.' (Actually, I'd had trouble with my shoulder, so it wasn't a complete lie.)

Nutty didn't buy it though.

'You're pissed aren't you!'

'No, no, Mr Davies…'

'I don't know what the world's coming to,' he muttered as he stormed off.

The following day, after all these preliminaries, the real highlight was to happen: Wales vs Ireland at Lansdowne Road. It was my first ever away trip to a Five Nations international, and I proudly took my place on the open terrace of that famous ground. It was a horrible day, the wind was howling and the rain was lashing. I stood with the boys, particularly next to Og, Rhodri Ogwen Williams, although he is better known to me as 'Homme' as he is the biggest queen I've ever met! He'd played the night before as well, and I think it was that trip that forged our friendship proper. Wales won that game, 12–9, and clinched the Triple Crown. We played France for the Grand Slam after that, but they beat us and we ended up sharing the Championship with them, the last time it was shared.

After the match we were due to attend a function at the Mansion House, I think in honour of the Welsh Colleges' team – can't be sure – all a bit vague, I'm afraid! The Homme and I were walking along the streets of Dublin on a damp evening trying to get to this place. We were wearing jeans, rugby shirts, and Welsh scarves, so no way would a taxi stop for us. Therefore, we tried to find our own way, optimistically sticking our thumbs out from time to time, hoping someone would give us a lift. And someone did. I'll never forget the sight of a Bentley pulling up alongside us. As the window wound down, we saw a very elegant-looking lady, possibly in her late 40s or early 50s, wearing very grand evening wear, sitting in the passenger seat. A big, well-to-do, handsome-looking chap sat next to her in the driver's seat, wearing a dinner jacket and bow tie.

'Are you Welsh boys?' he asked us.

We obviously said that we were.

'Where are you heading?'

We told him the Mansion House.

'Sure, we're going right past there, hop in.'

We had a lovely chat in the car about the game and rugby in general, and they dropped us off right outside the Mansion House. It was unbelievable that they did that, and just typical of the hospitality that I've always enjoyed in Ireland – maybe they knew I was an O'Shea!

We got back to Wales eventually, sometime in the middle of the following week. Back in college, Andy, who had organised the trip, called all the tour boys together in a lecture theatre. He asked us if we'd enjoyed ourselves and, when we said we most definitely had, he then asked if we'd like to go on a proper rugby tour next time. By proper, he meant for much longer than a weekend. We asked him where he thought we could go. His reply stunned us all. 'How does a six-week tour to the South Seas sound?'

There was rapturous agreement and howling of approval. From that moment on that tour became our focus. We organised loads of fundraising events, raising money any way we could. We even managed to get sponsorship from Fosters. So, a rugby touring team of students, sponsored by a lager company, left Cyncoed and went to Hawaii for four days, Fiji for six days, then to Australia for a few weeks, where the Lions were on tour. The Ireland trip had just been a warm-up!

9

THE BRITISH AND Irish Lions had always been a part of my rugby consciousness from a very early age. Obviously, that was because of dad being a Lion. I always followed the match reports and results of any Lions tour avidly. I remember when mum managed the Regent Hotel she would often stay over in one of the spare rooms, and I'd stay with her. In those days hotel rooms had big radios stuck on the walls, and that's where I listened to the 1974 Lions tour of South Africa, when I was a four year old. I don't remember the lines of commentary, but I do remember the occasion, sitting there with my mum listening to rugby on the radio. Therefore, the thought of being able to go out to watch some Lions Test matches – and that in Australia, where dad was – was just too good to be true. The fact that this would follow a few weeks of travelling around the world playing rugby with the boys, made it even better.

Only three freshers went on that tour, Paul John, John Luke and Jon Humphreys – so they had a great introduction to college rugby! Jon would, in due course, go on many rugby tours with Wales and the Lions. But whenever I see him now and we talk of that six-week college tour, he still says that he never went on tour like it!

The fundraising had been intense and full-on. There was a big gala dinner at the end which announced the raffle winners; it was quite an event as the main raffle prize was a Ford Fiesta. So someone had obviously donated such a vehicle to the rugby tour fundraising cause. As a result of donations and sponsorship, I don't think that any individual player had to fork out more than £500 each. That's not bad for a six-week trip to five countries.

The first stop on the tour was Amsterdam. Good start! We only had an afternoon there, but it was enjoyable enough. It was quite an eye-opener for me I must say, a 21-year-old boy from the Valleys brought up in Cornwall. I enjoyed the experience as a way of seeing something different, a way of sampling Amsterdam's unique cultural atmosphere!

We flew from Schiphol to Vancouver, and we were transported from the airport to our hotel in stretch limos. Not your usual rugby tour mode of transport! They weren't all the rage then, either, so it was quite special, and we watched WWF wrestling on the telly in the vehicle. Having checked into our hotel, we went to watch a game of cricket in a park in Vancouver, which I must say felt very colonial. The next port of call was The Jolly Taxpayer. It was my first taste of Americana: baseball on the telly, pitchers of beer, and popcorn on the bar. We then went to a pizzeria, before going back to the hotel quite tidily; we had an early flight next morning to Hawaii.

My arrival in Hawaii was not a pleasurable experience. A few months before the tour started, I'd had my 21st birthday. It had been a really nice occasion, which my mum went to town on, pulling out all the stops. My dad flew over from Australia too, which was really nice. Some dear friends, Mike and May Gordon, had bought me a good old-fashioned Australian-type cowboy hat called an Akubra. I thought I was the bees' knees in this hat, and had worn it non-stop on the first few days of the tour. When I got to the arrivals hall at Hawaii airport, I realised that I'd left it on the plane. I was gutted. I tried to put that behind me as we got into the next mode of transport Andy had organised for us. No stretch limos this time, but open-top jeeps which took us to the Aloha Surf Hotel, a block away from the main beach at Waikiki. We dumped our stuff in our rooms – I shared with Huw and Rhodri – and we all went out to enjoy Honolulu. It was my first taste of Corona beer, with the obligatory slice of lime in it, of course. In the corner of that same pub our tour captain, John Green, who'd played for England Schoolboys and would go on to play for Saracens, was sat with Leighton Davies and Don Llewelyn, the coaches. John was a non-playing captain, as he'd done his knee in just before the tour started. We might well have been a college renowned for rugby excellence, but the XV for the first game of an international tour was chosen in the corner of a pub and scribbled on a piece of scrap paper. Under normal circumstances, every single one of us testosterone-fuelled ambitious young men would have wanted to be chosen for the first XV. But, after only an hour and a half of being in the paradise that is Honolulu – surrounded by beautiful people, drinking this wonderful Corona beer with exotic fruit in it – priorities had changed. Each one of us started to think at various moments in that first 90 minutes that we would have to stop drinking if we were picked.

We were to play the Hawaiian State team in that first game. Greenie stood up to announce those unlucky enough to be chosen to play against them. In his usual Bruce Forsyth accent and manner, he addressed all of us. We would usually be waiting with baited breath to see if we'd been lucky enough to be chosen. This time, however, we were praying that our names wouldn't be called out. My prayers were answered. I could stay out on the pop all night!

I'll never forget the sight of the sun going down over Diamond Head that evening – it was stunning. The next day, the sunrise was equally breathtaking. Rhodri and I went straight to the surf hire shop to get ourselves a board.

Normally, I wouldn't go near the surfing fraternity. Rugby players and surfers just don't mix, as surfers have got long, blond hair and suntans, and rugby players are real men. That was certainly the case in my experience living in the rugby and surfing county of Cornwall. But on that tour, because of where we were, it was a case of when in Hawaii…

In the surf shop we pointed to a board we wanted. The shop guys looked at us and asked if we'd ever surfed before. Honestly enough, we both said no. 'In that case,' came the reply, 'you need one of these.' He pointed to a board about ten feet long. We weren't too impressed with that suggestion. We were politely told that, basically, we wouldn't stand a chance on a proper board, the smaller, all-singing all-dancing one we wanted. We listened and took the big boards to Waikiki beach. We paddled out to where the waves break, which in the case of this beach seemed to be about a mile from the shore. Paddling out there was hard work, hanging on as we did to our boards for dear life. Once we got to the waves, neither of us had a clue what to do! We were both fairly fit. We both swam a lot. But when that first wave hit, all of that came to nothing. We both fell off our boards and went under the water. When we came back up, the boards, at least, had managed to stay on the wave – and were heading towards the shore, back along the mile we'd just paddled to reach the wave. We swam back to the shore, only to realise that we couldn't find our boards. A quarter of a mile walk along the shoreline later, we found our boards. That was it. Back to the shop with an indignant 'have your boards back pal' look on our faces. But we tried, and the water itself was just amazing.

Game time arrived, and South Glamorgan Institute was ready to play the Hawaiian State team. The Hawaiian team were proposed to join Tonga, Fiji and Samoa in a South

Pacific tournament. Like all American rugby teams, the Hawaiian team contained big boys. But their understanding of the game itself wasn't that good. They didn't have the skills base. They depended on their strength in the scrums, with one or two of their backs able to be Jonah Lomu-type runners. We had a guy called Peter Cook on the wing. He went on to play in the centre for both Bath and Pontypool. On this tour, he inherited the nickname 'Bones'. He was wiped out in that first game. He chased back after a kick from the opposition, fell on the ball in the correct fashion, got up to clear it – and was absolutely 'emptied' by his opposite number! Cookie landed about ten feet the other side of the touchline, in the arms of his tackler. I've never seen anything like it. It turned out that this guy had been playing American Football for the Seattle Sea Hawks. The entire lateral aspect of Cookie's leg was burned off by the grass. 'Bones', as he then became known, spent most of the rest of the time administering lotions and potions to heal the ailments of the squad. The Hawaiians did enough to beat us that day, albeit narrowly. I suppose the fact that we'd spent most of the day on the beach sunbathing and mucking around didn't help our cause. We were true Brits that day, spending all day in the Hawaiian sun with no suntan lotion on. By the time we kicked off in the evening, we were a team of lobsters.

Next day, Leighton Davies called us together for a bit of a training run-through. With the hint of a sadistic chuckle in his voice, he told us to take our shirts off and get involved in a little one-to-one scrummaging practise. Bare, burnt shoulders rubbed against bare, burnt shoulders, as a grinning Leighton stood shouting, 'Push harder boys, push harder, full contact!' Sunburn was soon joined by grassburn, as we went through some severe dermatological testing. Luckily, we had a couple of days off before our next game against the Hawaiian Harlequins. So we hired jeeps and drove around the island, exploring beautiful coves and beaches. It really was a tropical paradise and we all thoroughly enjoyed ourselves.

However, we were pulled over by the police. Honolulu is a big naval port and American servicemen are regular visitors there. They spend a great deal of R+R time on the island, heading off to bars and clubs for long periods of time. And they quite often get into trouble with the local police. As it was the 1980s, most of us had really short hair with flat top, buzz cuts. There were five of us in our Wrangler jeep that day, including Huw and John, a big prop from Leicester. The three of us at the back were sitting on the bars around us, hanging on to the roll bar. A cop car came behind us with sirens blaring, and asked us to pull over. We pulled into a lay-by and John jumped out of the car, unaware of local protocol. The cops pulled out their guns and shouted at John to get back in the vehicle. Before he did they searched and frisked him, but he didn't take too kindly to such physical treatment. Luckily he kept calm and got back in the jeep. Having been reassured that we were Brits on tour, the police told us off for sitting on the back rails and said that we must sit properly in the seats. And off they went.

We played the Hawaiian Harlequins in one of the parks, a quite splendid location. Any panoramic view of Waikiki beach will also show Diamond Head, the imposing headland that dominates the skyline, just as Table Mountain does in Cape Town. In the shadow of this headland are many parks, far away from shops and bars. We played our matches in one of these parks as there were no rugby facilities there at all. We played on pitches that didn't have posts, even. They had soccer goals though, and any penalty or conversion had to be kicked over the crossbar and judged to have gone through imaginary up-rights. However, whatever the location, we lost our second game as well. We were a good few days further into our tour by then, and a lot more fragile. By then, no one gave a monkeys if we were picked to play or not.

The after-match shower was a case of running down to the beach and diving into the sea. The Hawaiian hospitality was superb and after both matches a fantastic barbecue was laid on for us. You're not allowed to drink alcohol in public places in Hawaii, but they smuggled some cans to the park, which would be far enough away from any prying eyes. Well, that's what we thought, at least. No sooner had the first cans been opened, than police quad bikes headed in our direction. They asked us what we were doing and we explained that we were on a rugby tour and had just played a game against the Harlequins. They were fairly understanding fortunately, and went on their way.

We headed off into town after that, to the local bars. We hit the Hard Rock Cafe, which just had to be done. No way could we leave the island without being able to say that we'd been to the Hard Rock Cafe, Honolulu. But I got bored after too long in one pub, and wanted to move on. Wherever we went we would sing, especially in a small pub called the Rose and Crown. We had a guy from west Wales with us: Mark Jeffries was involved with a male voice choir and so he was our leader. We would sing a mix of classics, like 'Calon Lân', along with the usual rugby songs.

As we left one bar and headed to another, the Butterfly Bar, I had a bottle of beer in my hand as I walked down the street, swigging as I went. I was very quickly approached by a policeman heading my way on a golf buggy down a pedestrian street. He had dark hair and skin. Approaching me in the golf buggy, looking as he did, I thought he looked like a well-known golfer, so I greeted him as such. 'Hey Seve! Where would you recommend we go to now then, Seve?' I think that might have antagonised the policeman a little. He looked at me, he looked at my beer. Looking me straight in the eyes, he said, 'Down it!' So I emptied the contents of the bottle down my throat in one. But something got lost in translation. He meant, put the bottle down. My act of obedience was actually seen as an act of defiance. I was up against a wall and being frisked quicker than I could say Budweiser. I was handcuffed to a palm tree while he called for back-up. The boys tried their best to plead with him, but it was getting nowhere. A squad car arrived, I was thrown into the back of it and taken to downtown Honolulu's police station. I had my mug shots taken there: front, right side, and left side; I was fingerprinted and then thrown into a cell. It was a classic scene from any film. The main room of the police station had a few officers sat behind desks typing out their notes, but in the corner there was an iron cage. And that's what I was thrown into. There were six or seven other guys in there, drunks and wasters, who didn't look too welcoming. I tried to start a conversation, but got nowhere. I did get a response from one huge guy near me, though. 'You say one more thing and I'll break your f*****g neck!' Needless to say, I kept quiet. I was then moved to a cell on my own.

The boys sent an official delegate from their midst to see how I was. Jon Humphreys, the fresher, had that honour. He arrived in a cab, having done a whip-round to see if he could bail me out. It took five hours to process the paperwork, but eventually I was set free. I was bailed for the princely sum of $25 and had to appear in court the following week.

The court hearing was set for a time which was after the departure of our flight to Fiji. So I had a dilemma. Should I skip bail? That was the obvious thing to do, as they weren't going to instigate an international search for me if I did. But we were due fly via Hawaii on the way back to Wales at the end of our tour. That could cause even more problems. So I phoned the court office to explain my predicament. They said that I'd be dealt with in my absence, and that the $25 would be kept as a fine. That didn't stop the boys winding me up when we flew back to Hawaii at the end of the tour, trying to make me doubt that the whole thing was over and making me think that I'd be arrested as soon as I got off the plane.

Fiji was our next stop. What an incredible place. Like many places in what's called the developing world, they have many beautiful and ugly things side by side. Poverty was certainly the ugly side of Fiji. I'd never seen such examples of poverty. We got there just after the Indian-dominated government had been overthrown in a military coup. We were staying with the army, who had a central role in the two coups that happened that year. This meant that everywhere we went, transported in army trucks, we were applauded and cheered enthusiastically.

We were staying at the Fijian army barracks in Lautoka. We weren't exactly spoiled for choice with restaurants, but we found a Chinese one we really liked. We went to the Moon and Seven Stars every night and enjoyed their food, washed down with Fijian beer. The food was prepared right next to what could only be described as toilets as dirty as those in the film, *Trainspotting*. But we survived.

We got up at five in the morning, showered, and then went out to train. It was too hot to train at any other time of the day. We played two matches in Fiji, with one of them against the army. When the army boys weren't working at their barracks, they'd be out on the field chucking a rugby ball about. We'd watch them quite often, and were all impressed by their rugby skills. They were very athletic and were amazing when running with the ball. A clear indication of the difference in resources between Wales and Fiji was the fact that the army team didn't have a pair of rugby boots for each player. They only had 14 pairs for the match against us. Both wingers had to share boots. One played barefoot in the first half, so that the other could wear boots, and then vice versa. With or without footwear, they were still too good for us and beat us.

The next game was in Nadi. There was a scrum during that game which was like no other scrum I've seen. On the flank for our team was a guy called John Leonard, who played a bit for Newport. The ball hadn't even been thrown into the scrum before John suddenly stood up and started running – straight towards the touchline, down the tunnel to the changing rooms, with a brown semi-liquid running down his leg! Every attempt to hold it in had failed miserably.

After training in the early mornings, we enjoyed everything that Fiji had to offer. The afternoons were certainly too hot for us to be outdoors much. Luckily, we came across a place called the Colonial Club. It was literally like something out of *It Ain't Half Hot Mum*. It was a white bungalow and looked like a gentleman's club, with all the stereotypes that's attached to such a place. They gave us temporary membership and we spent a great deal of time playing tennis, swimming, playing snooker and relaxing. It was unbearably hot, with temperatures reaching a 110 degrees Fahrenheit in the afternoon. I played a bit of tennis, but I couldn't last long in the heat, so it was then straight to the pool where I would find a corner out of the sun, lie in the water, and drink Coke through a straw.

Our last night on the island was quite special. Our hosts

At home in Hafodyrynys with John and Judy O'Shea, or mum and dad as I came to know them.

Nanna and Ganca – on the same day – with my mum's parents, Joe and Mavis Wilde.

At the age of two. Clearly my mum felt compelled to make me wear knee-high white socks to distract people from my outrageous cuteness… This was the high-water mark of my aesthetic appeal!

My very first rugby kit, St Erbyn's School. The stripes were chocolate brown and, rather appropriately, I'm sat outside the public toilets in Mousehole.

Surf's up at Sennen Cove, aged four. Shortly after this my mum was sensationally axed from the 'Baywatch' cast for refusing to remove her traditional Welsh daffodil swim cap.

Humphry Davy School, under-14 County Champions, 1982/83.
Back row (L–R): Dave Thomas, Tim Yendell, Phil Rich, Richard Brownfield, Alan Thomas, Steve Ward, Gordon Maddern, Tim Boston, Paul Osborne, Simon Humphreys, Paul Martin, Adrian Rutter. Front row (L–R): Mike Murphy, Paul Burgan, Richard O'Shea, Billy Peters, Tony Hands, David Coneybeare, Neil Dungey. Seated: Ian Robinson, Kevin Boase.

I was very proud to be the captain of Penzance & Newlyn Colts XV. This shot was taken just after the semi-final of the County Cup – we'd narrowly been beaten by Redruth Colts in Redruth. It was 15 February 1987 and our first defeat of the season, hence the gutted looks!

Back row (L–R): Roger Pearce, Roger Pascoe, Jan Oszewski, Tony Hands, John Lansley, Damian Kamara, Mark Murley, Mark Eddy, Phil Rich, Andrew Pascoe, Steve Cary, Gareth Manning, Andrew Blewett, Ian James, Richard Brownfield, John Bennett, Cecil Dunne.
Front row (L–R): Anthony Stevenson, Paul Osborne, Nicky Williams, Simon Stone, Richard O'Shea, Nigel Rowe, Lee Williams, Damon Horrocks, Gavin Rodda.

In my time at Penwith Sixth-Form College we won the County Cup in 1984, 1985 and 1986. The college provided nine players to the county under-18 schools' squad in the 1985/86 season.

Back row (L–R): Paul Burgan, Anthony Stevenson, Martin Haag, Steve Berryman, Billy Peters.
Front row (L–R): Richard O'Shea, Ian Luke, Simon Stone and Tony Hands.

Martin Haag went on to play many seasons for Bath RFC and was capped by England. Steve Berryman served in the Royal Marines and played for Combined Services vs All Blacks… Paul Burgan was later surgically removed from his shorts at Treliske Hospital!

I'm not sure what award I received from Mike Luke and George 'Bosun' James in 1987, but I'm certain it wasn't player of the year. That trophy was surely in the hands of Simon 'Dicky' Stone. He was some player and a great pal!

The Padfield family that has been so important to two, and now three, generations of O'Sheas. Here we are all together at my 21st birthday in 1989.

L–R: Chris Padfield, me, mum, Ellie (Padfield) Harries, Reg Creed, Zena Creed (formerly Padfield), David Padfield. In front: nanna and Avril Padfield.

I like to think that I've always had a sense of style. Day one of the epic S.G.I.H.E. RFC South Seas tour of 1989. In the back of a limo in Vancouver! Sion Wyn Davies, me and Marc 'Oz' Hughes.

Possibly breathing in… at the bar on Beachcomber Island somewhere in the middle of the Pacific Ocean, off Fiji, 1989.
L–R: Andy Macpherson, Mike Groom, me, Huw Davies, Rhodri Williams.

The team 'bus' taking us to the match versus Fiji Army. Game faces on! Mr Davies is in the shades, next to him Tony Copsey, John Luke. Nearest to the camera, to the right, is Paul 'Planet' Pook.

Welsh Student Rugby League World Cup squad – Australia, 1992.

Back row (L–R): Mark Isherwood, Matthew Lloyd, Matt Vail, Gareth Davies, Rob Appleyard, Stuart Jenkins, Chris Greenhall.
Middle row (L–R): Nicky Lloyd, Davey Malcom, Rick O'Shea, Byron Lloyd, Mike Jarman, Matt Donnison, Ben Smith, Wayne Phillips, Ashley Horrobin, Ioan Bebb.
Front row (L–R): Jamie Devonald, Dai Williams, Alan Hardman, Danny Sheehy (assistant coach), Clive Griffiths (head coach), Phil Melling (team manager), John Daly (captain), John Hughes, Ness Flowers.

The Cameo Club after the first refurbishment in 2001. I'm standing next to Luned Jones, Gwyn's sister. Luned joined the staff shortly after she returned from the USA where she successfully defended her 'world scowling title'! We had great staff and an awful lot of fun behind, and even sometimes on, that bar!

Summer 2003: Chad James and I raise a glass to toast our purchase of The Cornish Range in Mousehole. Chad, who is a shrewd businessman, quickly came to the conclusion that it would be a good idea to have a chef in the partnership! We were joined by another old Pirate pal, Keith 'Squeaky' Terry. He and Chad still own it; it's a cracking restaurant and well worth a visit.

'The Chimps'… well most of them… Out of shot somewhere are Paul 'Colossus' Collett and Rob 'Path' McNabb… well it was his wedding! These boys are the epitome of fun – just add beer and watch it all unfold! L–R: Paul 'Batton' Bainton, Stephen 'Whippet' Richards, Neil 'Lofty' Watkins, Christian 'Fliggy' Phillips, Craig 'Buddy' Blewett, LFB, Chad 'Jamo' James.

Serendipity Selfie! Ten years to the day that we filmed the very first grassroots item for *Scrum V* at Oakdale RFC in 2004, the same team, Steve Jenkins, Richard Bartley and myself found ourselves reunited at St Davids RFC.

Snowy Selfie! Rome in a blizzard! Myself and Ceri Jenkins at Italy vs England, 2012.

Old sea dogs, early December 2010. Filming an item for the rugby section of *Sports Personality of the Year* with Eddie Butler, Gareth Charles and Phil Steele.

Of all the items that I've ever filmed for *Scrum V*, the fact that I 'followed' England through the Six Nations 2013, is the one that people stop and talk to/heckle me about! You may recall Wales won handsomely that day... If I thought it guaranteed the same result every time, I'd wear the bloody thing every year!

Immediately after the great Welsh win over England, Phil Chapple, Ceri and myself enjoying the privilege of our jobs and treading the sacred turf... 'that' shirt firmly under the jacket!

I had the privilege of hosting BBC Radio Wales' coverage of the Six Nations 2013/14. Quite literally living the dream, with Garin Jenkins, 'Radio' Rhod Jones, Gareth Charles and Dafydd James.

Summer 2014: I was a surprise call-up to the BBC Wales coverage of Glamorgan's 'T20 Blast' campaign. We managed to maintain a rugby connection with this alfresco commentary of the Middlesex fixture played at Old Deer Park! Edward Bevan, Michael 'Pretty Boy' Powell and Ian 'Bolt' Thomas enjoying the fun in the sun. Glammy won, thanks to a superb century from skipper Jim Allenby.

I've picked up a few stories along the way, and am extremely fortunate to receive a fair few invitations to share them. On this occasion it was a lunch in aid of Prostate Cancer Cymru held at the Liberty Stadium.

Last-minute team-talk ahead of the greatest match of my life! Ushers Byron Lloyd, Chad James, Andrew Blewett and Simon Stone practise laughing at best man Anthony Stevenson's speech. Ant had a tough gig that day, which was also his birthday. He had to go on after my dad, but he knocked them dead and stole the show.

Gwyn Jones. This shot was taken on the morning of my wedding and Gwyn's expression can be explained by the fact it was a free bar.

The very definition of LFB! My beautiful wife Leisha on a very special day.

Leisha, dad, me and Marlene, at Heathrow departures lounge in 2006. They had come over for our wedding and we all had a wonderful time in the weeks afterwards. The goodbyes seem to get harder as I get older.

I may well look like Billy Bunter, but I think I was close to tears at this point! Graduation day for Dr O'Shea.

Johnathan and Michael at about six months old… Aww!

Birthday boys: John and Mikey, 5 October 2012, aged one.

The O'Shea Christmas card, 2012! I know… it seemed a good idea at the time… Me and Mikey, Leisha and John.

Mikey and John just minutes before their christening in October 2014.

And as a family, just after the service.

gave us a good send-off. They organised a lovo, a Fijian feast. They built a massive fire, placing rocks or huge pebbles on it, and left the fire to burn all day. After the stones were heated they were placed in a hole in the ground. Then chicken, lamb, fish and rice was added and everything was covered with palm leaves. This would then also be covered with earth and left for a couple of hours. When the hole was opened again, the food uncovered and served was unbelievable – the most incredible food I've ever eaten!

We were also served Kava. This drink is root based, with the root bashed and then sieved through muslin and served in a coconut shell. It looks like dirty dishwater. Drinking Kava is quite a ritual. Before receiving the cup from the person handing it to you, you clap your hands three times, drink from the cup, then pass it on to someone else, and clap three times again. It's known for its sedative and anaesthetic qualities. In other words, it's a narcotic! This ritual was far too similar to one of our Buzz Circle games for us to let that fact go unnoticed. So we decided to teach our Fijian hosts how to play Buzz itself. We all sat around a massive circle – there must have been about 60 of us. We got things under way, 'one, two, three, four, fizz…', but they weren't getting the hang of it at all. Their captain stood up and said that they wanted to teach us one of their games. 'It's called Bula,' he said, as he picked up a bottle of beer, which was a massive pint and a half bottle. He downed the whole lot in one, and then shouted triumphantly, 'Bula!' And then the next person stood up and did exactly the same, and so on. That was their game. Easy enough to pick up, and we joined in willingly. Drinking bottles of beer was interspersed with taking shots of Kava. So the raucousness caused by the beer was calmed down by the Kava.

I'll never forget lying flat on my back on the grass, Jon

Humphreys and Paul John beside me, beer in hand, looking up at the crystal clear, starry sky in this tropical location, thinking, 'This is pretty special.' And it really was.

10

THE NEXT STOP on the tour was familiar enough territory for me: Sydney, Australia. The first British and Irish Lions Test was scheduled for the Saturday after we arrived. Loughlin and I had to head to an Irish bar to collect our tickets, which was a really good start! The Lions were coached by Ian McGeechan and captained by Finlay Calder. The Welsh were represented by Ieuan Evans, Dai Young, Bob Norster, Mike Griffiths, Mike Hall, Tony Clement, John Devereux and Robert Jones. It was the first time the Lions had toured Australia since 1971 and the first time, since something like 1899, that they had gone there and not played New Zealand on the same tour. Unfortunately, we saw another record broken at the end of that first Test. Australia's victory of 30–12 was the heaviest loss by the Lions against the Wallabies.

On the Monday after the first Test we headed north to Brisbane, as Queensland University was the next fixture on our tour. The university had an amazing team, with the likes of Michael Lynagh in their ranks. The bus trip was epic, something like 16 hours, travelling through the night. We were rather shattered by the time we sat in a bar waiting to be assigned to a Queensland University player who would billet us for that leg of the tour.

What happened over the next few days is simply unbelievable, and is one of the best stories I've ever heard, but I worry that it will not read as well as it was told by Huw Davies, who was central to it! So if you are ever in the Cameo Club in Cardiff and want a good laugh, ask Huw to tell you about it; it gets better each time I hear it!

The entire squad had been allocated accommodation, with the exception of myself, Huw, Oz and Copsey. We sat with our kit bags, having a beer, when our lift arrived, and I recognised him straight away which is an important fact, because Huw clearly didn't.

'G'day boys, sorry I'm late.'

He politely declined the offer of a beer, had a quick chat with the Queensland University coach and came back to us.

'OK boys, Marc and Huw, you are staying with me; Rick and Tony, I'll drop you at my mate's house. Grab your kit fellas, the car's out front.'

Now, if I tell you that I was comfortably the smallest of the group, you can imagine how comical it was to see us all trying to get into the back of this bloke's Honda Civic with six weeks' worth of kit, and about four slabs of beer each that we'd removed with the permission of Carlton & United Brewery's Brisbane branch, as well.

Huw is about 6' 3", and he is considerably shorter than Copsey. Despite this, Huw insisted that he had to sit in the front seat 'on account of his knee'. We were pootling along quite nicely when Huw, who I think it's fair to say considers himself something of a spokesperson, began to engage our host and chauffeur in some polite chat.

'So, are you playing against us tomorrow night?'

'No, I can't mate,' came the reply in a polite manner.

'Why's that, you injured?'

'Ummm no, I'm in camp tomorrow morning,' came the reply, and you could sense that there would be no supplementary information.

'What, are you a scout or something?'

Our chauffeur had been backed into a corner and had to come clean.

'No, I'm with the Australian team.'

Huw looked at him now with a scrutinising eye.

'What, are you in the under-21s or something?'

'No mate, I'm playing against the Lions on Saturday.'

The next line is immortal.

'Who the f*** are you?'

I knew who he was. His name was Greg Martin. He'd played in the first Test and scored two tries and I think he won the man of the match award too, although, to be honest, it could have been Scott Gourley.

We did chuckle to ourselves at the back!

That, in itself, would have been a good enough story were it not for the events that then unfolded.

That night we all went out on the smash into central Brisbane, to the famous City Rowers. Oz and I made a call home to Wales and discovered that we'd been awarded our HNDs, like we needed an excuse to really get on it, but we did!

Oz and Huw had become thick as thieves during the season that had just ended before our tour. I think each other's 'no nonsense' approach to life in general appealed to both. There was one incredible episode which took place when we'd been out for a few one Sunday evening in Roath. A group of us were sat in the George when the bell for last orders went. Being a Sunday night we knew there were slim pickings for after-hours drinking, so we all mustered up as much cash as we had. We had enough for two pints each, and Oz was dispatched to fetch them. On his last leg back from the bar, he was carrying two pints in each hand, with his fingers dipped into the contents of each glass (a bit like one of those cranes that you put £1 into at an amusement arcade and it dips weakly into the box of goodies below, only to emerge with nothing!).

So as Oz was traversing the floor of the pub, some bloke bumped into him and he dropped the two glasses in his left hand. Huw let out an audible cry of terror with the realisation that 50 per cent of his beer had just gone on the deck! Oz, after remonstrating with the bloke, sat at the table and put the two glasses that remained intact in front of him, whilst fending off Huw's grabbing hand.

'I can't believe you dropped two pints!' Huw wailed as he reached for one of the remaining pair.

'Get lost mun!' or words to that effect Oz retorted, defending the two glasses in much the same way as a schoolboy encircles his exam paper to prevent a neighbour from copying his answers.

'These are mine, I dropped your two!'

Back to Brisbane, at the end of that evening / beginning of the following morning while waiting for a cab, Oz got involved in a scrap with some local boys. Huw, in helping Oz out of what he maintained was a viscous and unprovoked attack – yeah, right – had the sleeve ripped off his tour sweater. An episode for which he gave Oz an almighty bollocking. Oz then went into a plutonic sulk and told the taxi driver he wanted to go home to Blackwood and kept repeating something like, '23 Sunnybank Road, Blackwood.'

'Just ignore him, he's a congenital idiot,' said Huw, as he handed the taxi driver a piece of paper with Greg's address on it.

After ten minutes or so they pulled up at Greg's house, but Oz refused to get out of the car because he was not in Blackwood, and redoubled his instructions to the driver, who was quite understandably keen to get away from these lunatics by now.

Tempers began to boil and the volume grew, and lights began to come on in the street; it was about 4 a.m. Suddenly

Greg Martin appeared on his verandah in his dressing gown. He approached Huw and, being a part of the rugby brotherhood, had great empathy for the situation. He thought he could reason with Oz. Wrong! So he popped his head in through the open back door, only for Oz to think he was Huw, and so smack him one! Huw then smacked Oz, and it all got rather ugly, with the three men rolling around in the grass!

It was probably midday when the Welsh pair surfaced. Greg had already departed for training camp. Oz was still collapsed on the sofa. (I will spare Oz's blushes here, but let's just say that that particular piece of furniture will never quite be the same again.) Copsey and I pulled up in a cab to take us all to training at the university. Oz looked for his kit and, not being able to find it, declared that he must have been robbed, only to discover that Greg's girlfriend, in an act of uncommon kindness, had taken both Huw and Oz's kit and washed it all for them and that it was hanging on the line. Oz retrieved his kit, but sadly not without stepping in some cat mess on his way back to the house (which he then ran through Greg's lovely beige carpet). However, on his way out of the front door, he assured Greg's girlfriend that he would clean it up when he returned.

He never did, of course, because we trained in the afternoon, and later played the game against Queensland University. Afterwards we were invited to a massive post-match function. Oz couldn't attend this because it was compulsory to wear our tour uniform at such events. The uniform included the tour jumper and, as he'd torn the sleeve off Huw's, he had to give him his! I will always remember poor old Oz with his nose up against the glass as we swigged away on the free beer provided by our hosts!

Somehow, Oz 'got lucky' that night and didn't make it back

to Greg's. In the morning, with us waiting outside in the cab, Huw had to pack both his and Oz's kit. He was tamping, and when we arrived at the bus, he threw the kit at Oz, including a wallet and watch that he'd picked up off the bedside table. Huw then went to see Loughlin and stated that under no circumstances would he be willing to be billeted with Oz again.

And so to Toowoomba, and we gathered again to await our accomodation. Oz sheepishly approached Huw and apologised; they were great pals and so quickly resolved their differences over a beer.

'Oh, by the way,' said Oz. 'I didn't want to say at the time because you were so pissed off, but you gave me your wallet and watch.'

He handed the items back to Huw.

'They're not mine,' he said.

'Well, whose are they?' and then it dawned on them both...

In a little over 24 hours, they'd possibly offended this man by not recognising him, then assaulted him in the early hours, ruined his couch, walked cat mess into his carpet, and now nicked his wallet and watch!

On the field, the game against Queensland University was probably our best performance of the tour. They were an excellent team; they played in the top tier of Queensland rugby and would have been an incredible scalp to have taken. In the last minute of the match we were trailing, 9–4. Paul John, who's simply the best scrum-half I've ever played with or against, scored an incredible solo try. He picked up the ball from the back of the scrum near the halfway line, and sprinted and darted his way down the blindside to the try line and got back to score virtually under the woodwork! I can see it now, it was amazing, 9–8, but with a kick to come from under the posts. Even Nutty was smiling right up to the point when Mike Groom missed the kick that would have given us victory. Up until that point Mike had been known as 'Paparazzi Groom', because of his obsession with taking photographs of every incident on tour – he was like a bloody Japanese tourist. (He even got some shots of me when I was arrested in Hawaii.) We changed his name after that missed conversion though, and for the rest of the tour and all of eternity he is now known as 'Dusty' Groom, in honour of the England full-back who defeated Wales with a last-minute kick in 1980.

We left Brisbane and, as mentioned, headed to Toowoomba in Queensland, the garden city as it's called. It's about two or three hours inland from Brisbane. Coincidentally, one of my father's best mates from Randwick Rugby Club had moved to Toowoomba and bought a pub! I was billeted with him! We liked our stay in that town very much because that's where we had our first victory of the tour! We played Darling Downs University and, better still, I was the captain. The celebrations were of biblical proportions!

What a beautiful prelude to the second Test, one which has become famous in its own right, being affectionately known as the 'Battle of Ballymore'. The Lions' own website hail it as one of the most controversial Tests in Lions history. That just about paints the picture. They'd already lost the first Test and had been outplayed in every department. The Wallabies were buoyant. The midweek game before the second Test got off to a disastrous start, and they were losing to the Brumbies at half-time. But, inspired by Donal Lenihan, they rallied in the second half to beat the Brumbies convincingly, 41–25. That had a good effect on the Test team, as well. McGeechan, the shrewd coach that he was, hadn't been afraid to make big changes to the Test team, either.

He dropped five first-choice players, including Mike Hall and Bob Norster. Scott Hastings got his first Test chance, playing alongside his brother Gavin, the first time brothers had played in a Test together for the Lions since 1910.

Captain Finlay's team talk inspired the team in the dressing room and they ran onto the pitch fully fired up. But the Lions trailed for most of the match and were 12–6 down at the break. Two tries in the last ten minutes, by Gavin Hastings and Jeremy Guscott, snatched victory from the jaws of defeat. But the path there had been a bloody one. Flanker Mike Teague called it the most violent game of rugby that has ever been played. The flashpoint happened only a minute after the kick-off. Aussie scrum-half Nick Farr-Jones went to put the ball in the scrum. Fired up by his captain's speech, the Lions' scrum-half, the diminutive Robert Jones, cheekily stood on Farr-Jones' foot. And he erupted! The two smallest men on the pitch locked horns and the Lions forwards pitched in.

I now have the pleasure of working with Rob on *Scrum V* and I've heard him tell the story of that day many times at dinners, and if you get the chance to hear him, don't miss it, it's a belter! From that point on, it was carnage between the two teams. My father mortally feared that he'd lose his title as 'the only Lion sent off' which, at the time of it happening, had ruined his career. Now, some 20 years later, he was doing rather well on the after-dinner speaking circuit as the only Lion sent off, and really didn't fancy some young upstart stealing his thunder!

Luckily, the Lions ended with 15 men and won the match, 19–12.

If you check closely the footage of that match, you can pause the picture in a few places and see us Cyncoed lot clearly in the crowd. We had a massive banner that said,

'South Glam Institute South Pacific Tour, 1989: The Lions followed us!'

That was true, of course, as we'd left British shores a few days before they did. After the match, in rather euphoric mood after such a victory, we went to dig out John Devereux, a fellow student to most of us on the tour. He hadn't played that day, but he was a touring Lion. We met up and shared a good few beers with him; he was and remains a great bloke, old Dev's.

Our next destination was Surfers Paradise itself. We stayed in a beautiful hotel which soon became accustomed to the Cyncoed Buzz Circle. One circle game ended up with me having to go and stand in the middle of the hotel pool for half an hour without moving. John Hubbard had to stand guard to make sure I didn't move from my spot. And to make sure that he wasn't neglecting his duties, he had to shout, 'Halt! Who goes there?' on the minute, every minute. That was fun.

Not so much fun for Jon Humphreys in that hotel, though. He'd failed one of his first-year exams and had to take his resit at the hotel. The rest of us did all we could to encourage him, of course, and we didn't distract him in any way, shape or form. Right?

Training was great at Surfers Paradise. Nutty would separate us into two groups on the beach, maybe backs and forwards, or some similar grouping. While he worked with one group, the other would run across the sands towards the headland in the distance and then run back again. I reckoned that around 200 yards from where Nutty was standing was far enough to be out of his sight, so I mingled among the other beach users and bathers. Therefore, as the main body of the run pounded on to the headland, myself and one or two of the other more feckless players, probably

Homme Williams for example, would be porpoising in the waves having a great time, before joining the group at the back as it returned from its half-hour jog to the horizon!

Being sponsored by Fosters really kicked in on the Australian leg of our tour. Wherever we would go they would invite us to the local Fosters Brewery where we could stock up on our lager supplies; basically, as much as we could carry. It was free, but as they say, there's no such thing as a free lunch – we had to sing for our supper. At every brewery we would be ushered into the typing pool, where we would sing for all the staff who were there. Our choirmaster, Mark Jefferies, an immaculate little winger, would stand in front of us, having arranged us into an orderly crescent shape. We didn't sing the 'Four and Twenty Virgins' type of song though; we kept 'Calon Lân' and the likes for these occasions. And, before every Test match, food and beer was laid on for us for free.

Praise the Lord that we are a musical nation!

It was Sydney next for us and a match against Waverley, an eastern suburb in the city. The firsts played Waverley firsts and the dirt trackers played against their second team on the pitch next door. I played for the dirt trackers that game, and I was captain. Being in Sydney, dad was able to come to watch me play, which was not something that could happen all that often. We lost. Bummer. But, the biggest shame for us was not losing, but losing to a team which included a girl in the back row!

We were short of some players for our team as, by then, we were picking up injuries. So, Waverley loaned us some of their boys. Ten minutes before the end of the game they made a substitution, and on came a girl to take her place among the forwards. We were stunned. Needless to say, my dad has not stopped making fun of me for being in a team that lost to a team with a girl in it. My reply to that is that two international rugby players, Jon Humphreys and Tony Copsey, were also in that team. I might be wrong, but it does offer me some consolation! That was the last game I played on the tour.

The following Saturday the Lions were playing the third and final Test, so we had that to look forward to. The series was level at one game apiece and this was the big decider, following as it did the battle of the previous Test. It was another famous game – this time for the right reasons – as the Lions beat Australia, 19–18, and became the first Lions team to win a series from one-nil down. Ieuan Evans scored the only Lions try that day, following an ill-judged pass to our old pal, Greg Martin. It was good to see our fellow Cyncoed boy, John Devereux, on the bench, too.

I think the tour then headed to Newcastle University for a midweek fixture, but I stayed in Sydney to spend some time with the old man. With the squad strengthened due to my absence, they won that game before returning to Sydney for one last game against Sydney University. It was played on Sunday at the same time as the Lions played an Anzac XV. I really can't remember who won, I suspect they did!

Six wonderful weeks had come to an end and it was time to fly back home. I stayed on in Australia to spend some time with dad. Rhodri and Huw got off the plane in Vancouver, hired a car, and after Rhod got propositioned by a homosexual in the car park of Vancouver airport, they drove down the west coast, ending up eventually at Vail, Colorado. They played rugby there for about six weeks, alongside Lyn Jones, the Welsh international and current Dragons coach.

I knew that we'd never ever have such a tour again, even if we lived to be a 100. But more than that, I'm not sure that any rugby tour could be like that these days. It's just unheard of to go away for six whole weeks, across three continents, and throw in watching Lions Test matches along the way. Special memories and a hell of laugh!

11

I ALSO MADE another massive journey during my college days; I moved from scrum-half. The seeds of doubt sown when I went to Bisham Abbey as a schoolboy, and the telling words of my coach and friend in Cornwall, had come to fruition. I wasn't a bad scrum-half in that I could read the game pretty well and I had a good pair of hands. But I soon realised at Cyncoed that I was way too slow to compete in that position. However, the precise circumstances of the switch were still something of a shock.

As I said, I'd squeaked into the first XV squad on arrival, and I'd played a few games for the squad since that freshers' trial. As the end of my first term approached, we had a home fixture on a Monday night against Pontypridd. We often played against the old first-class clubs and, as previously stated, we usually came off second-best, but we lost this game, 58–0. There were four-point tries in those days, so this was one hell of a beating. Nutty was livid.

I think I shouldered more than my share of the blame for that defeat when the team sheets went up the following Thursday for the weekend fixtures. They always went up on Thursday afternoons, at about 2 p.m., and all the boys would shuffle out of the common room and have a look at the notice board. I looked at the piece of paper with the names of the first XV on it.

9. Richard Williams, on the bench, Stuart Jardine.

Bugger! Oh well, it was a hammering. I moved across to the team sheet for the seconds.

9. Nick Greenhall, on the bench, Richard Herborne.

Shit!

And so to the third XV…

9. Gareth Pugh, on the bench, Rick O'Shea.

F***!

I'd gone from the first XV scrum-half to the third team bench!

I was fuming, jumping, bouncing! I went straight to Mr Davies' room and knocked on his door which, in hindsight, was a mistake.

He called me in and I went to pull a chair to sit on.

'You planning on staying long, O'Shea?' he said with his trademark dryness.

'Well I was hoping to talk to you about the selection for Saturday.'

'Why, what's the problem?' he fired back at me straight away.

'What's my problem? Why am I on the bench for the thirds?'

His reply was quick and direct.

'Because we haven't got fourths!'

There was no answering that. He followed up by pointing out that I'd gained at least a half a stone in weight since arriving at college in September, and that I was pretty slow then.

'I'd probably need a calendar to time you over 100 metres now,' he chuckled.

'I'll never pick you at scrum-half for this college again, O'Shea. I'm going to give you a fundamental choice: you can either go into the back row or the front row, but if I were you, I'd cut out the middle man!'

I was somewhat stunned. I thought about it for a minute and resigned myself to my fate. Leighton was not a man for turning!

For some stupid reason I foolishly thought that perhaps some of my father's scrummaging genes might have been passed down to me.

'I'll have a go at tight-head, Mr Davies.'

'Good idea, your father wasn't a bad prop, we'll get you into the weights' room and get Mr Llewellyn to give you some scrummaging tips, and we've got this new training technique now called plyometrics.'

Well it was the 1980s.

'How flexible are you, O'Shea?'

'Well I can't do Thursdays, Mr Davies.'

And so that was that. From scrum-half to tight-head prop in five minutes, not bad!

It was a massive culture shock going from scrum-half to tight-head. I'd inherited my dad's physique but none of his talent or doggedness. I wouldn't say that I shied away from anything in the field, and I was more than willing to put my head on the line. But I don't think I had the mental courage to try to be a tight-head prop. That lack of courage was there because I didn't want to fail. So, on reflection, I now feel like I didn't really try. It was also the period when the whole idea of weight training was becoming much more important in rugby. By my time in college, pumping iron was really taking off, and rugby boys were beginning to look more like walking Groggs, most notably Matthew Lloyd!

Whereas I might agree that I needed to move from scrum-half, I'm not sure that the tight-head was the obvious answer to the problem. 'Don't die wondering' they say. Hooker would have been a better choice but for the fact that we already had two outstanding hookers at the college in Jon Humphreys and Mark Wysocki. I didn't consider being a hooker at the time.

Ironically, I did end up playing a season or two at hooker

for the Pirates. Our coach at the time, Bernard Durant, considered himself a radical thinker and decided he wanted to emulate the new strategy emerging from France and the southern hemisphere by picking three massive blokes in the front row. I was about 16 stone in my playing days, and either side me at our Mennaye stadium in those days was John Luke, my pal from Cyncoed who was about 17½ stone, and Nicky 'Baloo' Williams on the tight-head, who was 19 stone if he was an ounce! It was a flawed experiment, despite Bernard's best intentions, because I couldn't hook, and 20 years ago this was still a prerequisite to be hooker! On the one hand I could get around the field and link play pretty well, and I was also very good throwing the ball into the line-out.

I did have one more golden moment while playing hooker for the Pirates, in a match at home against Gloucester Spartans. It was a rugged but even encounter, with the scores pretty close as we approached the end of the game. We were in possession about ten metres outside the Spartans 22 in the middle of the field. I was stood behind the ruck and noticed that their full-back was missing. I called for the ball as first receiver. Their defence expected me to simply truck it up to their defensive line.

We used to get pretty good crowds at Mennaye; 500 or so even in those days. I heard every supporter groan as, instead, I chipped the ball over the defensive line. The groans turned to cheers, however, as they realised there was no one at home, and the ball popped up beautifully for me to run on and hand-off the covering winger to go over to the right of the posts!

At 27 though, that experiment was way too late to resurrect my rugby career. If I'd tried it at 19, maybe things could have been different. I obviously will never know, but that possibility haunts me now and again. Looking back, I can see that I followed the path of least resistance whenever I could. I was talented enough at rugby and life in general to muddle along and make a go of anything. But I hadn't really proven myself. I still hadn't really stepped up to the plate to do something for myself. Thankfully, that time would come. But it hadn't during grammar school days, and it didn't at college, either.

Playing in the front row also turned me into a frustrated player. At number 9, you're part of the game for every single minute, part of every phase of play, whatever it is. You're also a key decision-maker. Moving up front changed all that. I spent the best part of each game disengaging my head from my backside. Once my head was removed, I didn't get anywhere near the ball. That improved a little over time, and I learned how to become adequate at scrummaging.

All this frustration needed an answer, it needed to be dealt with. I found one by way of joining another rugby team – a rugby league team. A lot of disgruntled college rugby union boys turned to the league code at that time and I was happy to join them. I still played union though; I didn't defect totally. About 50 students would come to the college every year to do the P.E. course and there were other courses too, of course. There was only one first XV, so there would always be a surplus of really good rugby players. But the rugby league team wasn't only made up of the disillusioned. Some of the first XV union boys played league as well, as the game was becoming quite popular and appealing. Student rugby league was seen as a recruiting ground for the rugby league authorities, and they were putting a lot of money into that aspect of the game. At that time the senior professional rugby league code was densely populated by former Welsh rugby union international stars: Jonathan Davies, Adrian

Hadley, Rob Ackerman, Dai Young, Allan Bateman, Kevin Ellis, Scott Quinnell, Paul Moriarty and Gerald Cordle (who I later had the great pleasure of getting to know when he joined the Pirates, what a man!). And the list goes on. The former Scarlet and union international, Clive Griffiths, was in charge of the Welsh rugby league team, and they were doing very well.

There were only two student rugby league teams in Wales then, Swansea University and South Glamorgan Institute. The Welsh Students' team was chosen from anyone who was either a Welsh student or a student in Wales, whatever course, whatever college, wherever they came from. So, selection wasn't as straightforward as it might appear. I took to rugby league quite quickly, my hands proving useful. But I discovered that I was surprisingly effective in contact too, helped by being fairly low to the ground. The first tackler would often fall off me and then I could either off-load or just make good yards. Obviously, this suited the league game very nicely.

For me, personally, the pattern had been set. I was by then a prop, not a scrum-half. I would play union for Cyncoed on a Saturday, go out on the pop with those boys on Saturday night, get up on Sunday and join the league boys, and travel wherever they played, which sometimes could be as far as Exeter and sometimes even Hull!

I'd played only a handful of games for the college league side when Clive Griffiths came down to watch us play Oxford University one morning. After the game he asked me if I'd like to play in a trial for the Welsh Students' team. Perhaps he'd had a few the night before, as well!

The trial was a Student XIII vs Welsh Amateurs, selected from the few clubs that dared to play the 'devil's code' in those days, such as Aberavon Green Stars and, I think,

Crynant Pitbulls, although I may have made that one up! The game was played at St Helen's in Swansea, which was handy because it was right next door to Singleton Hospital. They might only have been 'amateurs', but they were rock hard! I was joined in casualty at Singleton by at least three others for stitches, which is rather ironic because it was at Singleton where I first became a medical student and was taught how to suture!

Bloodied, but unbowed, I was chosen to play for Wales. Hurrah! We were to play French Students as a warm-up game for their annual fixture against Great Britain Students, a fixture that had quite a lengthy pedigree. Before the match we were told that French Students had never been beaten on French soil by any team in the world, including the touring Australia and New Zealand team! That concentrated the mind. A good few of us in the Welsh team didn't have more than ten games of rugby league between us. We were to play the game in Nanterre, a suburb in western Paris, not far from where Racing Métro 92 currently play. We were put up in a hotel and our hosts arranged a civic reception for us the night before the game. There were posters heralding the event all over that part of Paris. The reception was a big affair, held in a huge hall with hundreds and hundreds of people there. I'd never seen anything like it.

We had one training session before the match. Clive had a specific tactic he wanted us to implement. Instead of carrying the ball for the usual five tackles, he wanted us to carry it for no more than two tackles, three maximum, and then kick it 'downtown', chase it in a straight line (in typical fashion), and press, press, press, but no penalties. And that's what we did. The French were not expecting it, and it threw them off their stride. We held our line and they couldn't get through us.

This went on for about 70 minutes, neither side giving an inch. I think we exchanged penalties and the score was then 2–2. Afterwards we broke out of defence; I think they dropped the ball and it was hacked ahead. I remember being close at hand as Gwyn 'Chuck' Morris, a goalkeeper from Porthmadog (like the rest of us chancing his hand at rugby league; he's now a first-class rugby union referee), dribbled it on over their line and scored the winning try. At that game I'll never forget the experience of standing proudly to sing the national anthem. This didn't happen at union student internationals – the players just walked onto the pitch and kicked off. But we stood there, in Paris, chests out, singing heartily, holding on to the Welsh badge on our jerseys as if our lives depended on it. The celebrations in Paris after the game, in what was in effect a historic win, were worthy of such a fine city. We headed home the following morning, our bus stopping at the obligatory hypermarket to pick up supplies on the way. I have very fond memories of Alan 'Abdominals' Hardman who was a great philosopher – well, he was that day – and Dai 'Dunvant' Williams, sitting with me at the back of the bus where all the bottles had been stacked. 'The font of eternal beer' we christened it because, no matter how many we drunk, the pile didn't seem to diminish! It was still going when we pulled into Roath!

We played Scotland next, at Widnes. That was the weekend of the Hillsborough disaster in 1989. We were staying in a hotel just outside Liverpool and played our match on the Sunday, the day after the tragedy. It's hard to describe the atmosphere that was permeating everywhere that day.

This is where my story comes round full circle. That summer, after our infamous six-week rugby union tour had come to an end and Rhodri and Huw had moved on to Colorado, I had to get back to York to play in the

Students' Rugby League World Cup. I'm sure that six weeks globetrotting on the pop wasn't the ideal preparation for such an elite event, but I did take my place in the Welsh team with all the others, a couple of whom, Richard Herborne and Mark Wysocki, had been with me in the South Seas.

We were in the same group as New Zealand, France and Holland. Yes, I know. We stuffed the Dutch, who I think might have just been in York on holiday and asked if they fancied making up the numbers! Actually, that is rather disrespectful. I think what actually happened is that they were the national Union side who stepped in at short notice due to the withdrawal of another nation; I think it might have been one of the South Seas nations. They had some very good players, but just no experience in rugby league and its structured way of playing.

The Kiwis were up next for us, at Oldham, and they won quite comfortably, about 27 points to 10. In the team talk before the game, Clive prepared us for something none of us had faced before, The Haka. He told us to pick out our opposite number and outstare him throughout the performance. I was wearing 10 then, so I looked out for their number 8 and stared at him hard. But he didn't know the moves for the haka, and was always a few steps behind the rest. So he wasn't looking at me at all, but looking at those around him so that he'd know what to do next. That diminished quite considerably my experience of such an auspicious rugby tradition.

Because of the events in Nanterre in February, the next game against France was a grudge match. They had a couple of full internationals. I remember one superb player, David Fraisse, their centre. Again, it was a pretty-close run affair, not much in it, until Dai Dunvant got yellow carded. (I think he nutted a Frenchman who'd done something off the ball.)

Anyway, being a man down proved too much for us and they won, I think, by about 14–6. I also dislocated my shoulder for the first time; it was an injury that would continue to dog me throughout my career. I therefore missed the play-off game against Ireland for fifth place; this was rather ironic because up until then that Welsh front row was comprised of an O'Shea, a Daley, and a Riley! We won that game quite comfortably.

These experiences served us well however, and with the growing appeal of the 13-man code (offering the chance to win international honours and win World Cups), it drew many more excellent union players to our ranks. Over the next few years we benefited from players such as Mark Bennett and Rob Appleyard, who won full union caps for Wales; Dai Manley and Matthew Lloyd, who became folk heroes in Pontypridd, and bloody good players like Dinlle Francis and Ioan Bebb also joined the ranks.

Each season there would be a European championship involving the home unions and France. I played against France about five times in all, and developed quite a friendship with my opposite number, Patrick Tagand, although we often had a few disagreements on the pitch! One year, while we played them at St Helen's, Swansea, a scrum went down on my opposite side. I was still on my feet, with Mark 'Socki' Wysocki hooking with his arms around me and the other prop on his knees, when one of the French boys took advantage of the situation and 'sent one through' before ducking away behind a colleague! Outraged, I went after him. Remember, I said that I hadn't inherited anything from my father's game. Well that's not true, because I inherited his inability to throw an effective punch! In a small-scale re-enactment of the Battle of Springs, I chased after this bloke, only to be picked off by the remaining five men of the French pack! And I got yellow carded! It was just before half-time, and when my ten minutes were up, Clive kept me off for the rest of the game. That's just the thing with rugby league: if you jeopardise the team by getting sin binned at a crucial time, that's it for you.

The team went on to great heights, populated mostly by Cyncoed boys who dominated the domestic scene. In those days student sport had three strands: university, polytechnic and college. We were a college and our rugby league team won the British Colleges' Cup for the four years I played at Cyncoed. The British Students' Cup was introduced and open to all student bodies (including polytechnics and universities) and we got to the final of that twice, both times against Loughborough University. We beat them at Headingley and lost the following year at Don Valley. In 1992, the Wales team beat France again, and then England, Ireland and Scotland, meaning that we were Rugby League European champions! That's something I'm quite proud of!

I'm also proud of the fact that Cyncoed's rugby union team won the British Colleges' Cup twice. As I said, I played both codes. We reached the final of that competition three times. The only time we didn't reach the final was as the result of a completely bizarre incident. We were due to play Bedford College in an early round of the cup competition. Off we set, in our bus, ready for that game. We saw a road sign that caused us a bit of concern. It said Bradford 50 miles. We went up to the driver and asked him where he was going. He replied that the destination was Bradford. We told him that it was Bedford College we were playing, and that he needed to turn round. He did just that, tearing down the M1. We didn't get to Bedford until about 3.30 and, as it was nearly Christmas, it was already fairly dark. We literally could only play ten minutes each way. They kicked a penalty goal and we lost, 3–0. It took some explaining later how the first team had lost to Bedford College. But we did win the whole thing twice and lost to St Paul's & St Mary's College, Cheltenham, on the occasion of the third final we reached. We were the best college in the UK for two years and second-best for a third.

The highlight of my union career came in 1991. We were on a good old-fashioned Easter tour down in Cornwall, to Penryn specifically. We played Falmouth in a 15-man game and then entered the Penryn Sevens on Easter Monday. While we were there, a call came through to us to say that the Welsh Colleges were going to play in a tournament on the Isle of Man, in a four-handed home union competition. At that time, I hadn't been capped in the union game at all, only in league. But I'd been chosen to play for the Welsh Colleges' union team in this competition. I was delighted.

After returning from Penryn, I was up and away to the Isle of Man in a minibus full of Cyncoed's Welsh students. We probably made up about 15 or 16 of the 23-man squad. It was a fairly eclectic bunch that chugged up to the north-west of England and then crossed over by ferry to Douglas, Isle of Man. I didn't play in the first game against Ireland. My old mate, David 'Jock' Morgan, who was Scottish but studying at Cyncoed, got the nod and played tight-head instead. If I'd been playing, I'd have been up against an Irish front row that contained Shane Byrne – known for his magnificent mullet – at number 2, but better known for going on to win 41 caps for Ireland and touring with the 2005 Lions. Incidentally, Shane has just made his acting debut in the movie, *Mrs Brown*.

I played in the next game, against England. Up against me at prop was a guy called Denver Jenkins, a Welshman who I believe was from Dunvant, and studying in England. I wound him up throughout the game, goading him about the fact that he was Welsh but wearing the rose on his chest. At a line-out or scrum I would say things like, 'I bet you didn't sleep well last night knowing you had to put that shirt on today.'

One of the non-Cyncoed guys in the Welsh team was Colin Gibson, who was studying law at one of the other Welsh colleges. He's the son of Mike Gibson, the legendary Irish and British Lion centre. Colin and I became friends, which is a nice piece of serendipity when you consider that our fathers toured South Africa together in 1968. He is now a lawyer in Gloucester.

To confuse the ethnic picture, the Welsh captain was John Green, who'd recovered from the knee injury that had prevented him playing on our South Seas odyssey a couple of years earlier. He captained both England Students and Welsh Colleges. Now, he was from Essex, and his team talk before the game was something else. He had to whip us up, as much as we needed to be whipped up before a game against England, his homeland. In an accent very similar to Alf Garnett, he urged us '... to whip the bastards. We hate the f*****g English; we must beat them and stuff them... you know how we feel about them in Wales...' It was as if he was reading Phil Bennett's famous speech before Wales played England in 1977, slamming what the English had done to Wales. You couldn't fault Greenie's commitment to the Welsh cause that day. The speech worked, and we beat England, the tournament favourites up until then.

We beat Scotland easily in the next game. In fact, it was such an easy victory that even I scored a try. I took a back peel from Greenie in a line-out and crashed over the line. Apparently, after the touchdown, I rose to me feet and uttered the words, 'I've done it Greenie, I've done it!' I'd scored a try wearing a Wales jersey. He continued to tease me about my triumphant proclamation for a long time afterwards. Ireland won the tournament, Wales came second, England third and Scotland fourth. All in all, we'd a good week on the Isle of Man and we accredited ourselves on the rugby pitch, too.

I took that jersey down to Penzance Rugby Club. That's where my dad's Barbarians shirt is, framed in a central position in the players' bar at the clubhouse. My Welsh Colleges' shirt was placed above the toilet door! By now, however, it's been moved to a more favourable position. I think they picked up on my displeased vibes!

Back to the rugby league World Cup in York. After the game against Holland, a man came up to me to ask if I'd be interested in visiting his club – again, my memory lets me down but I think it might have been Whitehaven – to play a trial match and possibly 'sign some papers'. I was very flattered. But I knew I needed to talk to Clive about it first. I told him what had happened and, once he'd finished laughing, he told me what he thought. 'Don't be so stupid, Rick. If you did go up there, the players would be thinking why was the club paying you and not their mate they'd grown up with. You would be a punch magnet for any of the opposition too, with them all wondering who the hell you thought you were, going up there to play. And besides, you're doing a degree; you have a cracking career ahead of you. Anyway, you're not hard enough!'

I got the message. I'm quite friendly with Jonathan Davies and John Devereux. We were often the canon fodder for the Welsh senior team at that time when they were training for Test matches. When we have a beer now, they remind themselves what a bloody tough sport rugby league was, and they couldn't believe that we played it for fun and not money! Which is an extremely good point, especially when you consider how supremely gifted they were, and how crap I was! Not that there is much comparison between the student league and the full-blown pro game.

By the time of the next Rugby League World Cup, I was coming to the end of my P.E. degree. That World Cup was in Australia; good news for me, of course. By then we were fully sponsored, with proper kit and a better organisation. I had to be fairly well organised personally too, as I went back home to Cornwall at the end of that college year. Training for the World Cup meant several round trips from Cornwall to Cardiff.

About two days before we were due to fly out to Australia, we were training in the gym at Cyncoed. The crash mats were out because Clive wanted us to practise the spear tackle (something which is now illegal). He wanted us to practise lifting an opponent up by the legs, knocking him on his back to the ground, and then following up by driving a shoulder into his ribcage with as much pressure as possible. Wayne 'Flumper' Phillips, a Cyncoed boy who was also in the Wales squad, did exactly what Clive asked him to do. He picked me up, threw me down and followed through with his shoulder – breaking my rib in the process. I knew instantly that there was no way I could show that that had happened. I would be replaced and not allowed to go on the trip. And no way was that happening. I joined the rest of the squad and flew out, in agony.

We were staying at the Australian Institute of Sport, a fantastic place in north Sydney. At our first training session there, during the contact session specifically, I pretended that I'd injured my rib just then. That, however, wasn't good. Up until then, I'd been more or less the first-choice prop. But because of my injury, they had to call someone else up in my place, a person called Matthew Lloyd. As soon as I saw it was him, I knew that that was curtains for me in terms of a long-term future with the team at that tournament. Another big pal of mine, 'Lloyder' was a superb player who played in the back row for Cardiff RFC when he was still in sixth form! He was a superb, promising young player, and super fit. The word prop doesn't matter so much in rugby league, and Matthew was usually in the second row where he packed down with future Wales international, Bob Appleyard. He was a superb tackler and runner and was one of those boys who was quick to appreciate that the game was changing; he'd already started to hit the weights big time.

Wales beat Fiji in their first World Cup game and then beat Samoa in quite a brutal game. Ioan Bebb scored a try and converted it for us to win 6–0. I became fit enough to play in the last group game, against Ireland, and we won that game easily. We were through to the quarter-finals. We knocked Fiji out, and next up was Australia in the semi-final. For 20 minutes we gave them a hell of a fright. Because a lot of us were rugby union boys, we could scrummage. They didn't expect that and they couldn't counter it. But scrummaging is not an important part of rugby league. They were superb, quick and well drilled, and they soon got to grips with us and put about 30 points on us. However, we weren't disgraced. Australia played Tonga in the final.

England and France had been knocked out in the group stages. We faced New Zealand in the play-off for third and fourth place. Boy, did we give them a game. At half-time we were something stupid like 25–0 up. We lost 27–25. We played like gods in the first half, but like clods in the second. I spent the day of the final in a bar at the Paramatta Stadium, as my rib had taken a turn for the worst in another game during the week of the knock-out stages. Myself, and three other Welsh boys, Flumper, Byron 'Byro' Lloyd, and Gareth 'Pubes' Davies, had been selected to play for a conglomerate of all the European sides against a similar group of all the southern hemisphere sides. Flumper and I were quite surprised at our selection, and assumed that it must be an attempt by the organisers to give some of the crap players a game. But that couldn't have been the case because Byro and Pubes were superb players. Pubes actually went on to play for Warrington first grade. Byro is still a huge mate, an usher at my wedding, and so I have to say nice things about him!

When the boys flew back home, I stayed out in Australia with my dad, as I'd done at the end of our six-week tour. This time Davey Malcolm, a fellow student and another big mate, stayed out there with me. I'd played against him when Wales played Scotland on the day of the Hillsborough disaster. After that game he'd become a Cyncoed student, and was therefore eligible to play for a Welsh college. As we'd both finished our courses by then, we were planning to stay out in Australia until about Christmas time and then go home to look for work. So we both went to the airport to wave goodbye to our fellow students. I had one last little trick up my sleeve. My stepbrother Paul works for Australian customs, so I had arranged for him to go up to one of our lads, tap him on the shoulder, and take him away for questioning. I'd set up Ben Smith. He came from Surrey but was a student in Swansea. He was taken to a side room, given a full search, asked a few questions, before being released to the amusement and ridicule of the rest of us.

Davey and I had a great time, working in all sorts of jobs, mainly in the brewery trade because of dad's contacts, but also in a Cash & Carry. By November, dad had a new job. Powers were a big brewery in Brisbane, and he was offered a job as their general manager. That meant he had to move house, so I decided to come home early.

The Welsh Students' rugby league team had done very well that year. We were European champions and had reached the semi-final of the World Cup. That gave quite a momentum to our game when the team arrived back in Wales, and I think it helped the game generally in south Wales, too.

That was the magic of places like Cyncoed and Trinity. They offered you a chance you wouldn't get anywhere else: an opportunity to play good standard rugby and even the chance to represent your country. All the boys at such colleges, but especially at Cyncoed, were good rugby players, at least up to county level. Some were internationals, and we had a chance to play alongside them and gain even more experience. It's unfortunate that those opportunities are not there for those coming through the system today. Those little idiosyncrasies of Welsh rugby, such as first-class clubs giving the likes of South Glamorgan Institute players opportunities to play in midweek fixtures, have unfortunately gone.

12

WHEN I STEPPED off that plane from Australia in the November after our World Cup experiences, carefree college life was now firmly behind me. I needed to work out what I was going to do with the rest of my life. I hadn't told mum that I wasn't staying out with dad till Christmas, so I drove to Cornwall and surprised her with my early return. It was a pleasant surprise, thank goodness.

Throughout my time in college I still regarded Cornwall as home. I went there during college holidays and I still played games for the Pirates when I could. But I lived in Cardiff for most weeks of the year. And I loved it. But there was one problem. If I went back to Cardiff, who would I play for? I couldn't play for the college any more. Whereas in Penzance, I had a team I could call my own. And my family was there too, as well as all my friends.

So I settled back into the Cornish way of life. I got a job with my mate Jimmy Richards' building firm, labouring for them on various projects until Christmas. After Christmas I started to look for jobs in earnest. I bought the *Telegraph* every Thursday, for the appointments section, and pored through it avidly. One thought channelled my search for a job. In my last year at college I shared a house with some other boys, including Huw. By then he was a rep with a drug company, and some of the other lads in the house were teachers. I could, therefore, compare the two occupations. Teaching looked like bloody hard work, and reping seemed to have greater scope for fun. Such profound thoughts influenced the way I read the *Telegraph* every Thursday.

I started applying for drug rep jobs. I dialled a number to enquire about a position, and they put me through to a recruitment firm who interviewed there and then over the phone. Now I can talk, make no mistake about that, but I wasn't ready to be questioned just then. So when they asked me why I thought I would suit a career in sales, I intended to convey the fact that I considered myself to be an excellent communicator. But, what I actually said was more along the lines of blabbering gobbledegook. Not a good start. In fact, at the end, there was polite sort of, 'Well, thank you for your application, Mr O'Shea. Don't call us, we'll call you.' I never heard from that company again!

But I was more prepared for the next telephone interview and had answers at the ready. I told them that I had previous sales experience, which was an adaptation of the truth surrounding a summer job I once had with the National Trust at St Michael's Mount in Cornwall. I was basically a talking signpost, directing people as they disembarked from boats or traversed the causeway if the tide was out to various points of interest on the island. The rest of the time I'd stand at the end of the quay, practising my golf swing with a rolled-up National Trust umbrella. However, there was an aspect of the job that did involve asking people if they wanted to join the National Trust, and directing them to the appropriate officer if they did. That, as far as I was concerned, was sales experience, and that was how I sold it.

By this time I'd been in contact with Huw who'd told me the basics of what they wanted to hear:

'Tell them how you explained the features and benefits of membership.'

'The what... how?'

'OK, look, a feature of membership will be that they'll enjoy free access to National Trust properties, right?'

'Yes.'

'Well, that access is a feature.'

'Right.'

'The benefit is that they'll never be bored on Sunday afternoons, as they'll have access to over 1,000 venues across the UK to which they can take their families and enjoy a wonderful day out, absorbing the culture and history of this great and historic country.'

'Oh, I see, it's all about bullshit!'

'Bingo! And, O'Shea, you have more at your disposal than most.'

Huw's advice was gold. Royce Recruitment Agency invited me for a face-to-face interview at Heathrow airport. While I was digging a hole in Leedstown for Jimmy Richards' crew – alongside my long-term drinking partners from Mousehole, Blewett, Wiggy and the Doddsies – my mum went to Marks and Spencer to buy me a new suit, and then drove me to the interview held at one of the hotels on the outskirts of the airport. I changed into the new suit in the hotel toilets and off I went.

I was directed to an area where the interviews were held, and signed in at the desk and was offered a coffee and told to take a seat. I remember sitting in a leather Chesterfield, doing the *Telegraph* crossword, in the hope that it would make me appear intelligent.

The interview itself was conducted in a bedroom which had had its furniture removed and was now set up as an office. My time came, and I walked towards the bedroom door and knocked on it. The door opened, and a very attractive young lady stood there in front of me. I reached out my right hand in order to shake hers and I said, 'Hello, I'm Richard.' But she was actually standing to my left. There was a mirror on the wall by the door and I greeted her reflection! What a good start.

But I made up for it in the actual interview which was conducted by her. She was happy with the fact that I had a 2.1 degree and could speak confidently. She arranged a final interview with the man who would be my direct line manager if I got the job. The position was with Reckitt & Coleman, a very large, well-known household company. Reckitt's were the chemical side of the business, and Coleman's were more on the mustard, Robinsons Barley Water; they own many household brands such as, Dettol, Lemsip and Mr Sheen. My next interview would be at their Dansom Lane HQ in Hull.

What an incredible building! It's an imposing Victorian redbrick building with equally impressive features inside. There was no shortage of marble, oil paintings, carved wood, high ceilings and alcoves. There were enormous portraits on the wall of all the former directors of the company. A guy called Roger Turnell interviewed me. He was a big fella, balding, but with a neatly-trimmed beard and a kind face. He called me in and sat me down and began the interview with a few questions. Then, after about ten minutes, he picked up my CV and said, 'So, you're an O'Shea and you're from Cardiff.' I said that I was, but had actually grown up in Cornwall. I didn't expect his next question. 'Are you any relation to John O'Shea?' I said he was my dad.

'How is the old bugger?' Ever so slightly taken aback, I told him how dad was and that I'd not long ago seen him in Australia. It turned out that Roger Turnell used to play for Northampton in dad's rugby playing days.

He then asked me what I really knew about sales. I told

him honestly that I had a mate who was a rep, and that I realised that the job was all about building relationships, but that I had no real direct experience of sales. I assured him that with good training I'd learn what was needed. He agreed and offered me the job. I was a Reckitt & Coleman employee. My mum's nickname for me since has been 'Lucky Fat Bastard' or just LFB and, to be honest, that's what I wanted to call this book, and it was a contender at one time! The way I got the job, and the bounty that came my way in subsequent days, was the catalyst for why she called me that!

About a week later I was sat with mum in the post office when a driver delivered my company car. A little later Barry Cornish, the postman, popped his head round the door with a recorded delivery letter containing my company credit card, and in the afternoon mail a cheque for £500 arrived so that I could open a bank account to use as a float for business expenses! I then went on a ten-week training course at HQ in Hull. At the end of the first week I drove back home because it was Easter bank holiday and we had a packed rugby fixture list. But, to be honest, that drive was a bit of a ball ache. However, I did enjoy parking my company car in the clubhouse car park, feeling as proud as an extremely well-endowed dog. Actually, most of the other lads had nicer cars than mine, but this car was the first that I could call my own, even though it wasn't, of course!

I stayed at a hotel in Hull on the other weekends, which worked out fine as the rugby season was drawing to a close anyway. That gave me an opportunity to go and see the football team I'd followed since I was at school, Leeds United, or 'Super Leeds' as I like to refer to them! They'd won the old football league division one in 1992, which was the pinnacle of Howard Wilkinson's revival of the club after years of wallowing in the second division. I saw them in their first year in the new premiership league. I'd waited all my life to see them play. Crystal Palace were their opponents that day and it ended as a 0–0 draw. What an anticlimax! I've seen them play about half a dozen times since, but have never seen them win unfortunately.

My patch as a rep was Cornwall and east Devon, taking in Plymouth, Torquay, Brixham and Sidmouth, but it didn't extend as far as Exeter. I lived at home for the first few months, but then shared a house in Callington, near Plymouth, with a friend who has already featured in this book, John Luke. He was a Cardiff boy who'd done the same Human Movement Studies course at Cyncoed as me, and then got a job as a rep in Devon and Cornwall. Another former college student and England Schoolboys' cap, Jason 'Bungle' Barton, moved in with us a little later on. The three of us played for the Pirates. Lukey, as previously mentioned, was a prop. He was a Welsh Students' cap and I think he played a bit for Bridgend. To be honest, it was because he was a better prop than me that I moved over to hooker! The three of us had an enormous amount of fun!

This was the beginning of the period when Dicky Evans took a central role at the Penzance & Newlyn club. A hometown boy who went away to university – I believe he studied Engineering – Dicky then worked in Kenya where he became a very successful businessman. He'd played for the Pirates, and developed an affinity for the club which would never leave him, and I certainly believe that he always had the club's best interests at heart when he invested a considerable amount of his fortune there as the professional rugby era dawned. Like any story which affects tradition, I'm sure that there are many who might disagree with that.

As I've suggested, what happened in Penzance after 1995

is not difficult to explain to anyone in Wales because it's so close to what happened in Welsh rugby – both examples are just different economies of scale. In much the same way as the WRU understood that Wales couldn't sustain 12 professional teams, Dicky Evans understood that the professional game in Cornwall could not be represented by just Penzance & Newlyn RFC, so he sought to make it representative of Cornwall as a whole. The Cornish absolutely love their rugby, of that there is no doubt. When there's a county game, the stadium is full, and if they get to the county championship finals, they can three-quarter fill Twickenham even. The RFU loved Cornish involvement in those finals as it guaranteed bums on seats. In an attempt to galvanise that potential support, Dicky Evans changed the club's name to Cornish Pirates and promoted plans dedicated to building a new, more centrally-located stadium within the county.

Notwithstanding this, the players that Dicky introduced enjoyed success on the pitch and they flew up through the leagues. During my last year with the club, Mark Ring was appointed player-coach, and he brought a number of top-quality players at various stages of their careers to Cornwall, including Kevin Moseley, Gerald Cordle, Chris Mills, and Mark Roderick. Joe Bearman was just starting out his career when he joined us from Newquay. Martyn Madden also arrived. I'd been informed that our scrummaging needed reinforcing – like that was a newsflash to me! I must confess that Martyn might not have seemed the obvious choice to achieve that goal, but I think he finished as top try scorer! He was such a good player. At the end of his season with us, Llanelli Scarlets called him back to their squad and he scored the winning try in the Welsh Cup final.

Big money was being invested and a team was being

built for success. They were unquestionably exciting times. Surprisingly, there was a chat about 'terms' for me, but I certainly wasn't going to sign up as a full-time pro because I had a pretty good job by Penzance standards. The rep job required some work in the evenings, which meant that I couldn't always attend training, thus rendering the next level of contract difficult to commit to.

From day one Dicky Evans faced two fundamental problems. Firstly, as I've alluded to, parochialism is as rife in Cornwall as it is in Wales. He was very unlikely to get the 'dyed in the wool' St Ives or Redruth season ticket holders to put allegiance to their team aside and now follow a 'rebranded' Penzance team. The second barrier to Dicky's ambition was the fact that he needed the support and/or approval of the council to get a new stadium built. As much as I love Cornwall – and I do cherish the time I spent there and the people that I grew up with, and I hope that has come through in these pages so far – it's not a progressive place and, down the years, I've been desperately frustrated by the influence of the naysayers and the NIMBYs that populate the county.

Cornwall's industry and ability to provide employment has either been lost, in the case of mining, or emasculated by legislation, in the case of farming and fishing. It does have incredible potential as a tourist destination, but it took the authorities about 40 years to approve the plans that linked up sections of the dual carriageway that now runs through Cornwall. I mean, Sweet Baby Jeebus... come on! Spookily enough, since they did, places like Padstow and St Ives are now among the elite holiday destinations of not just Cornwall but the whole of the United Kingdom. For the last 15 years, at least, there have been plans to turn the old Penlee Quarry between Newlyn and Mousehole into a marina, but the opposition has been so vociferous that it still hasn't been done. I'd have thought that any scheme that can regenerate what is effectively a hole in the coastline and offer the potential of employment, if only during its construction, would be welcomed!

I also feel that sport has been short-changed in Cornwall, possibly because its participants aren't involved in politics; they're too busy playing sport! I've already given you a roll call of great Cornish rugby players, but they love football and cricket too in Cornwall. I think that when you consider the money that's been invested in other cultural enterprises there, it's an insult to all those boys and girls who populate the playing fields of the Duchy that the county council couldn't find a way forward in conjunction with Dicky Evans, to build a stadium for Cornwall that would easily be accessible to all, somewhere in the middle, probably around Truro. I think that, in all probability, the ship has sailed for the Pirates. Rugby needed to be represented further west than Bristol and it seems that the Exeter Chiefs club, with their well-run set-up, now meets that need.

Back on the field of play, as I said, my shoulder kept popping out. I'd been having trouble with it for a while but it gradually got worse. There was increasing pressure on us to turn up for training, particularly as the club was now paying us to do so, therefore the stakes were higher. It was all proving difficult for me because of work commitments and the increased pressure on my damaged shoulder. I was with the Fisons company by then, having been made redundant by Reckitt & Coleman after about 18 months. They gave me three months' notice. I had an interview the week after with Fisons and I got the job. I also received about £10,000 severance pay from the company. So that worked out quite well I'd say. LFB.

I was interviewed for the job at Fisons by a chap called Paul Chard, an ex-Cyncoed student. But he didn't mention that fact until well after he'd wound me up by making some scurrilous slur that the college was full of drunks and wasters, and that it had a reputation for that throughout the college world! I started to get defensive and told him that when I was there I was surrounded by elite athletes who were proud of their abilities. He then turned to me and asked, 'You don't remember me do you?' and then proceeded to tell me that he was at Cyncoed as well, and that he remembered me there. He even mentioned that I was called 'Bargain Bucket' (I ate a KFC meal for four on that trip to Dublin). I got the job and learned all I needed to know about repping from Paul. He's the one who taught me how many beans make five.

Almost as soon as I got the job – in fact I was at the training course – I dislocated my wrist playing in the County Cup semi-final against Launceston. My employers had words with me about that, telling me that as I was on a training course such an injury didn't matter so much because I could be taken from place to place. But, if it had happened while I was working proper, on my own, then it would have been an entirely different matter. In no uncertain terms I was given the choice of either working or playing rugby. I would be of no use to them if I had to take time off because I was injured. I was nearly 28. I could have kept on playing, as technically they couldn't stop me. But my priorities were changing. Work was becoming more and more important. The demands of playing for the Pirates were becoming greater, too.

As I'd always done throughout my life thus far, I had a niggling thought in my head about this whole situation. Was I in effect using the Fisons ultimatum as an excuse to cover the fact that I knew my playing days were coming to an end, anyway? Did their comments make it easier for me to accept the inevitable, in fact, deflect the inevitable? I'll never know for sure, but I suspect that I probably did just that. Their words were conveniently timed and I made the most of them. Either way, my rugby playing days were over. I'd never had any illusions that I'd pull on the red jersey of Wales, not once. But I still wonder if I could have played regularly at a level higher. I have to bring myself back to that mantra, 'Don't die wondering'!

I enjoyed an enormous amount of fun as a Pirate. When they played in the higher leagues, we toured quite a lot around the clubs of the south-west. We didn't exactly travel in style, though. Our on-board toilet facility was about 12 foot of garden hosepipe with a funnel banged on at one end. We would close the bus door with one end of the hose outside the bus and the funnel end inside. Going for a pee meant standing in the bus stairwell and aiming for the funnel which would carry the liquid along the hose and deposit it on the road. We would arrive back in Penzance in time to get ourselves to one of the nightclubs.

Or, more often than not, the Alexandra Inn, which was about a nine iron from the Pirates club. The Alex was quite simply the greatest place I've ever known. It was run by Ian 'Smudge' Smith and his long-suffering wife, Pat. I look back on those days with such fondness. It was a cracking boozer with a sensational jukebox. Nightclubs were not for me really; I love music but I also like to chat, and get served!

Lock-ins at the Alex were the norm, the jukebox was eclectic, the pool table 'winner stays on', JD and Coke the mandatory forfeit for defeat. I bought a lot of JD and Coke. By three in the morning, those still standing would take part in the World Spoof championships until around 4 a.m., when Smudge would play the VHS of the 1989 Littlewood's Cup final that was won by his beloved Luton Town, before unlocking the jukebox, and putting Peter Starstedt or Roger Whittaker on for a final sing along.

There were so many times that I woke up on the pool table at about 9 a.m. on a Sunday with a '... a ship lies rigged and ready in the harbour, Tomorrow for old England she sails...' or 'You talk like Marelene Dietrich and you dance like Zizi Jeanmaire...' on repeat, while Wendy Stirling pushed a hoover around the bar, a room which not only had furniture on its floor, but also half a dozen of the Pirates first XV!

It would be impossible and unprintable to recall all the fun and mischief we got up to in those grand old days, but all the characters that are important in my life now were mostly there then: people like Joff, Buddy, Dicker, Raazaq, Marty, Bicky, The Savages, Squeeky, Patch, Willow, Dave (how come he doesn't have a nickname?), Tarts, Whippet... it's an endless roll call of great pals with whom I share wonderful memories, including the summer fun playing cricket for Penzance, skippered by little Treve Laity.

I guess that when you are an only child you do collect friends, but there are two lads that have become much more than friends. Both of them will be absolutely mortified that I've been asked to write a book, both even more so if I declared in this book how much they mean to me! Anthony Stevenson and Chad James are boys with whom I've shared so much and could certainly publish a lengthy memoir of the fun we've had together.

One such night was very portentous. We'd played away in Gloucestershire, and just about made it back for last orders at the Bosun's Locker. I was chatting away with Paul 'Ozzy' Osborne and Richard Nicholls, when my eyes fell on an incredibly attractive young lady. I didn't know who she was.

It turns out that I knew two of her sisters, Clare and Amanda. They were twins and were going out with my mates, Adrian Bick, the captain of the Pirates first XV, and Anthony. But I didn't know Leisha.

She came up to me at the bar and asked me if I wanted to dance. I looked round to see where Chad and the rest of the boys were, convinced it was a set-up. But she appeared to be serious, so I took her up on her kind offer. We danced to 'Dancing in the Dark' by Bruce Springsteen. I love Springsteen, but I'm an awful dancer. Leisha was deeply amused, laughing at the shapes I was throwing. (She assures me now that she was laughing with me.) We got on really well and started seeing each other. She was 18 and I was about 26, which I guess was quite a gap, but it didn't seem like it. It just seemed right. We've been together ever since. We married in 2006, on the twelfth anniversary of that first night, and I could probably fill the pages of another book describing the fun and the challenges that we've faced, as you'll see. What I must say, however, is that she is a quite remarkable lady, albeit with poor taste in men!

As a wife she is supportive but not unquestioning. While she has backed all my varied schemes, she has often taken some convincing. Leisha is unquestionably the ying to my yang. Where I am chaotic, she is ordered; where I am flighty, she is dependable. She is incredibly stylish and effortlessly elegant and I'm incredibly proud that such a beautiful, kind and loving woman has chosen to be my wife and mother of my children.

13

I LEFT FISONS after about a year with another redundancy package, having already secured another job with one of the world's biggest drug companies, Merck Sharp & Dohme, or MSD for short. With Reckitt & Coleman, I'd been selling Gaviscon; with Fisons, eye drops. And with MSD I was part of the team launching statins, a drug to combat high cholesterol. I wanted to be involved more at the cutting edge of developments, and with MSD I was. The company car was better too, a BMW this time.

But, the working environment was quite a culture shock. It was alien to every environment I'd worked in up until then. I was offered promotion at one stage. A week later, I was asked to make a presentation at a meeting instead of a colleague who was off-sick. Unprepared, I gave the presentation. In it I referred to the fact that we weren't doing so well in certain geographical areas. I explained that these gaps could possibly be the result of hospital consultants in those areas not being aware of the drug in question, because, as yet, it was not on the formulary – the list of drugs permitted for use in those hospitals. Meaning, that the whole area would be undersubscribed with the drug, as the way the system worked depended on consultants using the drug first. Then, that would filter through the system to GPs and other practitioners. So if a drug wasn't prescribed in a hospital, it was unlikely be used anywhere else in the area. That's where the work of the hospital rep came in. The hospital rep of our company at one particular hospital put in a complaint about my comments, claiming that I was undermining his efforts. That was certainly not my intention.

My boss phoned me to discuss the issue and said that she wanted me to submit a daily report from then on, noting exactly what I was doing and where. I queried the inconsistency of one minute putting me up for promotion and the next treating me like a trainee. There was no budging on her part. Around about the same time, the annual sales conference was being held in Sardinia. On the last evening, after the gala dinner, we had a chance to let our hair down. I hooked up with a few of the Welsh boys and we started singing some Welsh classics. Everyone else seemed to enjoy themselves. The MD of the company and a few of the senior staff came over to listen. After a while the play list dried up, and I left the group with one or two others and headed for a bar down the road. As I walked away, one of the senior managers came after me and told me that the MD wanted me back to sing some more songs. I politely declined, but the guy looked at me very disapprovingly and told me that the MD wouldn't be very happy. In fact, nobody said no to the MD. I basically replied that I was a sales rep not a monkey, and carried on. Later that evening, one of my mates came up to me and said that my response wasn't the correct one, and that it would be seriously frowned upon. He added that my card was probably marked. I have no patience with that sort of corporate mentality at all.

But, luckily, about two weeks beforehand, I'd been approached by Astra – before their merger with Zeneca – asking if I'd like to work for them selling respiratory products. At the time I was happy with MSD and heading for promotion, with no intention of leaving the company. But, things had changed. So, after returning from Sardinia, I phoned Astra and asked them if the job was still open.

It was, and I started with them some time later. I enjoyed my time with Astra, forming great friendships with Nick 'Beamer' Evans and Paul 'Goat' Irwin.

However, by now, my plans were changing. I'd been invited to Huw Davies' stag do in Bath. While it was a fairly posh affair – as such weekends go – we managed to put a fair few away. Rhodri Ogwen Williams was also there, and one evening while very much 'in our cups', we rekindled a dream that we'd had many times as students: owning a bar. The seeds were sown, and soon I was plotting my way back to Cardiff. I discussed the possibility of an internal transfer with Astra and, to be fair, they said they'd consider the proposal should any opportunity present itself. But, given that Huw had worked in Cardiff for Astra for nearly a decade and was one of its best reps, it seemed unlikely that his position would become vacant!

Rhodri by then had done very well for himself, working for S4C and then moving on to be one of the main anchors for Sky Sports. The three of us got talking and an idea was hatched. Rhod and Huw were both very settled in their chosen careers, to the point that neither could give up the 'day job', but they both wanted someone that they could trust to be the hands-on partner. By now I was more than happy to give up repping and fulfil that role. The plan was in place and a search for the right venue began. The first few properties we looked at were entirely inappropriate and they would have bankrupted us within two minutes.

Fate once again smiled on me when my former boss Paul Chard's wife, Vicky, who was a regional manager for a company called Parke-Davis, got in touch with me to enquire if I'd consider moving to join her new sales team in Cardiff! LFB!

I would be selling a new statin and I'd also be working

with the god of all reps, Meirion Roberts. Meirion had been capped by Wales in the 1960s; he'd played with dad at Cardiff RFC, and was coach of the very successful Cardiff Medical School rugby team. He was the Pelé, the Barry John, and the Muhammad Ali of medical reps, having done the job since the late 1950s, and effectively written the book.

Leaving Cornwall behind after nearly 30 years was a difficult thing to do, but I knew that I was going to somewhere equally warm and friendly as, for about six months in the summer and early autumn of 1999, I moved into a flat with Chad and Buddy! Another book could be written about this period alone!

During this time Leisha remained in Mousehole, working as a nanny for our friends, Dave and Jacquie Roberts. She'd been looking after Zachary for about three years and did not want to leave them in the lurch. So she stayed on in the job until the time suited both parties for her to move on. Leisha has always been so dedicated to the families she works for.

While I was waiting for her to join me in Cardiff, I reprised my student lifestyle! Both Chad and Buddy had been playing for the Pirates on pro terms, but felt that the time had come to leave Penzance to pursue new horizons. So they were sharing a flat in Marlborough Road, Roath, when I joined them and we had some incredible times which intensified in August when we all joined Llanishen RFC! I played only about six games for the 'Mighty Llan' but I loved it, and made some great friends: Rob 'Path' McNabb, Paul 'Batton' Bainton, Christian 'Fliggy' Phillips and Paul 'Colossus' Collette; known collectively as the Chimps. In the intervening decade, from Kinsale to the Costa del Sol, from Liverpool to Taunton, but mostly in the 'Diff', this random collective has been central to some of the best times that I've ever had.

It was the middle of the night at Marlborough Road when Chad woke me up to tell me that I had a call from Huw. He wanted me to meet him the next day, as a business had come on the market and he thought it would be ideal for us. It was the Cameo Club in Canton, or Pontcanna... if you're an estate agent! It suited us down to the ground and we bought it. I gave up my job with Parke-Davis, although I did feel very guilty about letting Vicky down, as she'd stuck her neck out for me gambling on brining a rep from Cornwall to work in Cardiff. I'd only been with them for about six months, but had earned enough of a bonus to part-fund my end of the deal to buy the club. I made up the balance with a loan from a friend who I won't name because it would embarrass him, but he knows who he is. I repaid the debt within 18 months, but I will never forget his kindness, or his faith in me.

We created the Pontcanna Pub Company and formally took ownership on the first day of the Rugby World Cup in Cardiff in 1999. Word had got out – largely because we'd been telling everyone for about six weeks – that we'd taken it over, and on that first day we were absolutely ram-jam full to the rafters. Huw got all the medics and reps involved; Rhod brought his media friends. It couldn't have been a better start.

The Cameo Club in those days was a completely different place to what it is now. The place has a fascinating history. During the Second World War, Cardiff, like so many other areas of Wales of course, was bombed. The Riverside Conservative Club was one of the casualties of the bombing. They relocated to the building that is now the Cameo Club. They were granted a licence to function as they had in Riverside, and when their former home was rebuilt, they moved back there, with the premises in Canton still keeping its licence. It has stayed open ever since, in various guises. It was known for its 'closed-in look'. The entire façade comprised of glass blocks that proved impenetrable to light! I always used to equate it with the Winchester Club in *Minder*. It was always a private members' club, and somewhere along the way it was granted a 2 a.m. licence. There used to be a tiny dance floor in the upstairs bar, the existence of which the licence depended on. When I say tiny, I mean tiny. If Adam Jones and I were dancing at the same time, there would be no room for anyone else! It never did 'live' entertainment because of the noise, being an end-of-terrace property.

It had been run by a very impressive lady called Barbara Rees, or 'Babs' as she was known. She was a legendary Cardiff figure. She was always on the door of the club. But there was never an admission fee to come in; you just had to buy a raffle ticket. But, of course, there was never a raffle. It was always full of great local characters, which gave it a unique atmosphere. I still wrestle with my conscience a little as to what we actually ended up doing to the Cameo, however genuine our intentions were. It did occupy a specific place in Cardiff's folklore and had a role in that community. When Huw, Rhod and I took the place over we had big ideas. We were entitled to those ideas, of course, because we'd bought the place with our own money. We thought we knew what Cardiff needed. Rhodri, at the time working for Sky, was in London a lot and was familiar with places such as the Groucho Club and Soho House. I think we thought, and hoped, that we could make the Cameo something like that. It was only in the fullness of time that we realised that Cardiff didn't want something like that. It didn't want exclusivity. It just wanted somewhere where you could go and have a quiet beer. When we got there, I think people paid something like a fiver for membership. By the time I left the Cameo, they were paying £50 a year.

There was still a perception, however, that people weren't too sure what went on behind those glass blocks. Was it some kind of speakeasy? What actually was happening was that people came there for a quiet drink, often late at night, many of which were BBC or NHS staff after a late shift. They didn't want to go somewhere to get smashed; they just wanted to go somewhere quiet and anonymous after work for a drink and a chat. I think I can count on the fingers of one hand, in the three years I was there, the number of times that no one came into the Cameo of an evening. It was licensed for 140, with 80 allowed downstairs and 60 upstairs. We would quite often have to open the upstairs even on a Thursday night.

The worst day of my life was in 2001, the first time (after we took over the club) that England played Wales in Cardiff. From the second our doors opened, we were already full. I was on the door with a clicker counting people in and out. I was in the horrible position of having to refuse entry to people who were members, and explaining that membership was no guarantee of entry as we had rules to operate by. That's never a pleasant or easy thing to do. I had more than my fair share of abuse on such busy occasions, even being punched and spat at – and that was just some of the women.

Add to that also the fact that we were always under pressure from two or three neighbours who didn't like having such an establishment on their doorstep. So things could get very fraught. The early days were difficult in terms of knowing who was who, and who we should let in. We did honour Babs' membership system at the start, of course, and then drew up our own, incorporating hers, before it was pretty much just our membership list in the end. But there was an overlap. I remember many a night people would come to the door and be asked if they were members. The reply quite often would be, 'No, no, I'm in *Pobol y Cwm*.' Of course, eager to please and not offend, I'd let them in. But this became something of a regular event. One night, in particular, it got daft, one after another, again and again:

'Are you a member?'

'No, *Pobol y Cwm*.'

After about the sixth time I morphed into Basil Fawlty:

'Oh, *Pobol y Cwm*, of course! Do come in. Do you want some sandwiches while you're here or perhaps a bottle of champagne?'

The club was full of characters – some of whom were as colourful as the day was long. People like Don, the local lollipop man, who patrolled the road near the Robin Hood pub round the corner from the Cameo. He was a decorated war hero who always wore his medals. He'd come in and ask for his pint in an old-fashioned dimpled glass, kept just for him. Don's mum was a Russian opera singer. He was Cliff Morgan's brother-in-law. He was a real character who always turned up immaculately dressed in his blazer and tie. That is, apart from Friday nights, which was party night, when he'd come in wearing a massive sombrero. He always carried his certificate of citation with him, as well. He used to be a steward at the Arms Park back in the day when my father was playing. So when dad walked into the Cameo, having brought a party of Australian supporters over for the World Cup in 1999, Don was sat at the bar:

'Jesus, it's the Count,' dad exclaimed.

Apparently Don was known as the Count of Monte Cristo. I've no idea why, but they hugged each other and shared a beer. That was really nice. Everyone loved Don and that's largely what the Cameo was about.

Then there was another character called Twm Gwyn. He was a classically-trained Shakespearean actor. He was a dark-haired Welsh speaker and a passionate nationalist. His life's work was a thesis about Saunders Lewis. He had an incredible voice and quite often after he'd had a few beers, I'd call him over and say, 'Twm, Twm, come here, come and do "First Voice" for me.' He would then launch into a very Burtonesque rendition of Dylan Thomas' words, which was incredible. On the other end of the scale, he did a stint on the extremely popular soap opera, *Crossroads*. Understandably, that completely messed up his Shakespearean acting credibility, and when the TV acting dried up, he became a floor manager at the BBC. He also worked for us behind the bar at times, which was quite a common occurrence among our regulars. Twm has unfortunately passed away, and one of my biggest regrets is that, as he died after I'd left the Cameo, I didn't get to hear of his passing so I missed his funeral. I most certainly would have gone if I'd known.

Don, the lollipop man, was one of the people, along with rugby stars like Jonathan Davies and Gwyn Jones, who'd have to make an annual trip to the council offices on our behalf to counter objections raised about the Cameo by one particular person. The next-door neighbour, who owned a restaurant, objected regularly to the noise level at the Cameo, even though he'd been a member before he bought a restaurant. We'd have to appeal every licence renewal rejection on the basis of these noise objections, but we would always win thanks to the support of the members mentioned and many others. But we were ordered to take steps to try and reduce any possible noise interference, which meant, of course, spending a lot of the money we were making. One year we must have spent something like £20,000 on sound insulation.

That meant, of course, that it was reducing the amount of money we were making from our investment. As I was living above the Cameo and managing it – being salaried for my work, in that sense – I got something back. Rhod and Huw however, made nothing at those times when we had to pay out for alterations, adjustments or improvements. We made enough money in our opening six months – which coincided with the rugby World Cup, the Millennium celebrations, and the Six Nations – to pay for a part refurbishment the following summer. This phase one refurbishment would turn it into the funky place we thought Cardiff needed. So none of us made anything from the fantastic start we had.

We did try to keep some elements of the Cameo as it was under Babs' management, though. The Wednesday night darts team, for example, and the use of the club as a sort of HQ for Clwb Rygbi, the rugby team of the city's Welsh speakers. We kept on Mark Rees, the barman, a Canton boy, who knew his trade and the club so well. But still, some of the locals mistrusted us, thinking that we were going to completely change everything. We didn't do that, but possibly we did change it more than was necessary. The Clwb Rygbi, for example, stayed with us for a while but then moved elsewhere. They had free reign in the upper room in Babs' days as no one else used it. But when we started taking bookings for functions in that room, we had to ask Clwb Rygbi if they minded not using it on certain nights. They understandably got fed up of this uncertainty and left. As did the darts team eventually. These kind of changes were happening as the Cameo was restyling its identity.

As certain regulars left, we were establishing a new and different customer base. People from the television industry and the Welsh-speaking community had always been the clientele, but now other professionals, such as doctors and lawyers, were becoming Cameo regulars. From a business point of view this was certainly the right decision. But on a human level, I'm not so sure.

When we first bought the club Leisha worked in Cardiff for about four or five months as a nanny for a family of business people. We were living in the converted attic above the Cameo; I used to have to lock her in at night on Fridays and Saturdays because you could access our rooms from the upstairs bar! I know, she's a lucky girl! Her job in Cardiff came to an end when the family moved away. As our residential status was less than ideal, she had the great idea of taking a job in London and working for one of the wealthiest families in Britain and earning more money than I ever have! This is again typical of Leisha's dedication and support. She could easily have protested and demanded that we moved to a more suitable home. Instead, she remained positive and adapted to the situation, ultimately putting us in a better position. I was living rent-free above the Cameo, with a company car. OK, it wasn't the Lexus I had with the drug company, it was a second-hand Rover estate! A good Cash & Carry car! It became known as the 'Comedy Car' when Rhod borrowed it one day to drive to Barry and the horn got stuck every time he took a right turn!

The club was evolving. We put big French doors along the whole of the front of the club, opening it up from the dingy glass blocks look of old. We opened during the day as well, opening at lunchtime, tapping into the growing café culture of the time. We wanted to make it an all-day venue, not just a late-night drinking venue.

The next step on that road was opening at nine in the morning. That did change the working day significantly, especially for me. We would close at 2 a.m. but not everyone would be out until about 2.30, going on 2.45. Then there was the clearing up and cashing up to do, which meant sometimes getting to bed about 4 a.m. Often a member of the day team would let us down, so that meant that I'd get up at eight to get everything ready for the 9 a.m. opening. That would happen quite a lot and it became quite difficult. Running your own business, eh? Be careful what you wish for.

It was difficult for the Cameo to be all things to all people at the start, and it took time. But it did work and we were very successful. The great and the good of Welsh performing and broadcasting were now our people. Christopher Walken made an appearance at the Cameo once, on my night off! The young Rhys Ifans was an early customer, as were Richard Harrington and Mark Lewis Jones. So was Gethin Jones, but he was just Clwb Rygbi's scrum-half then! Even Jill Douglas came down to do a celebrity stint behind the bar during one international day. We asked the senior mixologist from London's Groucho Club to come down for a week to teach our staff how to mix cocktails. We could offer whatever people asked for, virtually. We would get the people from Gordon's to come down to teach us how to make a perfect gin and tonic. (Which, by the way, is to put the ice in first, pour the gin slowly over the ice, put lime around the rim – not lemon – and top it up with Schweppes tonic, no other. That was useful to learn, I've perfected that one.) Such evenings were great fun and proved to be very popular, largely because we gave a lot of stuff away for free as they were sponsored by the brands. But, through all this, as much as the glitz of it all did appeal and work for some, there was still the underlying feeling that all people really wanted was a place to go for a pint or a glass of wine.

The personal toll on me was proving to be increasingly difficult. Initially, my only day off was Sunday, when the

Cameo was closed. The fact that Huw and Rhod wanted someone they could trust to run the club was understandable and necessary. I'd also invested in the Cameo, so I was safeguarding my money as well. But, on a personal level, it did mean that I had a massive time commitment to the place which, in effect, was taking over my life. I began to get the feeling, by nature of my day-to-day circumstances, that I was working *for* Rhod and Huw and not *with* them. That got especially difficult for me when we had our directors' meetings, with the emphasis – real, or simply perceived – coming from them of 'what are *you* going to do make this place busier, more efficient and more profitable.'

In business terms, it's an understandable and reasonable enough question. However, I'm not sure that the boys always fully appreciated the implications of what they wanted done. I knew the place was working pretty well, but I wasn't sure what exactly I could do to get the place banging on a Monday night! I was feeling the pressure, of that there is no doubt. There was a time when all that put a strain on our friendship and went a long way to verifying the saying, 'don't go into business with your friends'. Eventually, there were a series of regrettable episodes that culminated in me handing in my notice. I'd resigned from positions before, but never from my own company. It was made clear to me that I couldn't hold my post as director of the Pontcanna Pub Company if I wasn't working behind the bar. I think this confirmed the fact that I wasn't considered an equal. After three years at the Cameo, it was time for me to move on. The friendships between us were undoubtedly diminished by this experience. This was clearly very sad; we were all very close. I'm godfather to Huw's youngest daughter, Holly. Happily, enough water has passed under the bridge for us to have put it all behind us. We get on just fine now, and Huw was extremely helpful when I returned to medical sales in 2005, and again when I needed advice on how to get into medical school. Rhod is now based in Qatar and is back on form with Al Jazeera. As a trio we don't see as much of each other as we might like, and whilst things didn't go well for us in business, I think life is too short for grudges to be held for too long.

Huw and Rhod bought out my share and, always something of a slow learner, I used the cash to buy a restaurant with Chad, the Cornish Range. I used to wash dishes there as a kid in Mousehole, but in the intervening years it had undergone a transformation from café to AA Rosette and then a *Michelin Guide*-listed seafood restaurant with rooms. My partnership with Chad proved to be a better experience. The business had its moments, as they all do, but the friendship never wavered. Soon we were joined by another old mate from our Pirates days, Keith 'Squeaky' Terry, as it did seem that if you owned a restaurant it would be a good idea if one of us was a chef!

From the summer of 2003 I would act as front of house and barman Monday to Thursday, and then travel back to Cardiff to meet up with Leisha for the weekend when she returned from London to the apartment we now owned in Cardiff. I was also appearing on *Scrum V* by now, too.

Chad bought me out of the Cornish Range under very different circumstances in 2008, knowing that I might need the money to put myself through medical school. So, in a very real way, the Cameo proved to be a pivotal period in my life, as witnessed by the simple fact that, had I not bought the club, I would never have become a doctor, nor would I have worked in broadcasting.

14

I MET A number of people from the sports department of the BBC when they came to the Cameo for a quiet drink, and also rugby players, old and new, of course. It was at this time that I first met Gwyn Jones. I'd often join the boys at a table in the corner, fascinated by their conversations, especially about the mechanics of broadcasting. Producers, reporters and commentators alike would find a willing audience with me whenever they wanted to talk shop. This fascination could be traced back to the mists of my Cornish days.

Like many people at the age 17 or 18, I hadn't been at all sure as to which direction I wanted my life to go. I'd always been drawn towards rugby broadcasting. Living in Cornwall, your only contact with the best top-flight rugby – or any sport come to that – was through television or radio. Timing added significantly to geography as well, in that I was watching sport at a time of unsurpassed masters of TV commentary: rugby with Bill McLaren, tennis with Dan Maskell, snooker with Ted Lowe, and cricket with John Arlott and Richie Benaud. Each one of them, craftsmen with words. So, just as a player I wanted to emulate rugby stars on the pitch, in turn I looked up to these broadcasters with awe. I probably realised that I wasn't going to reach the top playing rugby, but as my ability to talk greatly exceeded my ability to play, perhaps there was hope!

These thoughts came right to the fore when I hung up my rugby boots for the last time. I was in my late 20s and Saturday afternoons were now free for the first time in two decades. What on the earth was I going to do with all that spare time? Thoughts of broadcasting whirled round and round in my head. In the end I phoned my pal Rhodri Williams. This would have been about two years before we both ventured into buying the Cameo Club. At that time, Rhodri was anchoring Sky Sports News, and the channel was beginning to break into rugby coverage. Rhodri was also among their leading rugby presenters.

I asked him what he thought I should do to get into broadcasting, knowing as I did that Rhodri didn't have any journalistic training, either. However, he felt that, as his dad was one of the directors of S4C, he'd been given an insight into knowing what was what in broadcast media. I asked if he thought that going to college for formal training was a good idea. Rhod thought that at this early stage that might be a bit of a radical step, and suggested instead that I go along to a local newspaper or radio station to see what they could offer me. That way I'd get an idea if I was any good at it, before making the pretty big decision of going back to school. It proved sound advice indeed.

I went along to the local newspaper, *The Cornishman*, and spoke to another old pal called John Williams, who'd been unfortunate enough to play outside me at fly-half when we were with the Pirates. 'Willow' had in fact gone back to school himself, at the School of Journalism in Cardiff, one of the best. He'd lived with me and the boys on Kimberley Road for some time when he did that course, and was one of the great drinkers of his time. He said it would be OK for me to write a feature article as some sort of trial. I decided to write a story about one of my oldest and dearest mates, Steve Carey, a former team-mate of mine at the Pirates. By then, 'Wiggy' had met Bettina, a stunning Mediterranean beauty who was at college with his brother, Phillip. They'd married and moved to Gibraltar. He'd earned his way into the Gibraltar national rugby team. Steve also represented the Rock at cricket in the ICC qualifying tournaments for the World Cup proper, and had played in some exotic locations, including Singapore and Hong Kong, against teams such as Kenya and Holland. I wrote a feature on the Mousehole boy who through fate and hard work became a double international for Gibraltar. It was printed, and I had made my debut! Despite the interesting subject matter, it was as clunky, clumsy and long-winded as I am!

Next stop, Radio Cornwall. A chap called Dave Martin was their main rugby man. Dave was a true gentleman and heavily involved in Cornish sport. He was a schoolmaster who coached various levels of age-grade rugby. He had a lovely West Country lilt which added to his appeal as a commentator on rugby matches in Cornwall. His work as a teacher ensured that he had good vocabulary and use of language. I arranged to meet Dave for lunch at a Falmouth hotel, and asked him the same questions that I'd asked Rhodri. Here follows another Lucky Fat Bastard story! 'Funnily enough,' he said, 'in two weeks' time I'm going to New Zealand with the Cornwall under-15 cricket team and I'll be away for two weeks, so there'll be a gap in the schedule. Come down to the radio station and we'll give you a voice test and see what's possible from there.'

It went well enough for me to be given a chance. I was told to be at a Pirates match the following weekend, doing match updates into the sports programme. I was perched above that magical tunnel that had so excited me when I ran through it as a boy, and I must say there was something quite nice about starting off my broadcasting career reporting on a team I'd only finished playing for a few months earlier.

That familiarity with the locals, though, proved to be a double-edged sword. Then, as now, when you cover games for radio you are given an ISDN kit which plugs into a specially installed phone line at the venue to ensure a very high sound quality, superior to that of a standard phone line. There's no real mystique, you just plug the line in and dial up the studio on the box. This line stays open all the time and the producer at base will simply fade you up when he wants to put you on the air. Everything was going quite well. I'd delivered a 'scene set' and my first updates, but was mortified when the line suddenly dropped off and I lost contact with the studio in Truro. I tried to redial but nothing happened, it stayed dead, no lights would come on! In desperation I checked that the line was still plugged into the kit. It was, and so I followed it along its path to the socket under the stand. I peered over the tunnel only to find Colin 'Dumbo' Dymond, a local legend from his playing days, beaming up at me with the other end of my ISDN line which he'd pulled out of the socket in his hand!

'A' right O'Shea?' he beamed at me. 'Testing... testing. Can you hear me?' he said into the other end of the line as though it was a microphone! He plugged it back in and I got back online, no harm done!

When Dave returned from New Zealand, they kept me on, and I continued to provide updates from various games in the county every Saturday for the rest of the season. I also got called back at the start of the following season before I moved back to Cardiff. All in all, I worked for about 18 months for BBC Radio Cornwall, and loved every minute of it. A few of those games stand out in my mind quite clearly.

For example, the day Launceston played St Ives on Grand National day. England were also playing Ireland in the Six Nations. I was given the radio car for the day, having had a quick course that morning on how to use it. I drove from Truro to St Ives, and parked it where St Ives play, Alexandra

Road, which is situated on top of a massive headland that looks out over the bay to the Atlantic. I extended the aerial mast out of the top of the car and managed to get online as required. The game unfolded and I started my work, watching and making notes for my updates. I then heard a message in my headphones:

'Umm... OK, Rick, we've just lost our BBC Five Live feed from the Six Nations game and Aintree. All we've got is you and the radio car, so you're going to have to do live commentary on the rest of the match.'

Wow! Live broadcasting... you've just got to love it! I was so excited. Then they asked if I could see anyone around who could provide a 'second voice' for analysis. LFB... Graham Dawe, former Bath and England international hooker and then coach of Launceston, was patrolling the touchline. I didn't know him well, but I think he saw the desperation in my eyes and took pity on a front-row colleague. I'm not sure that Eddie Butler and Brian Moore needed to be all that nervous, but the two of us took charge of broadcasting the game and it was a triumph! Luck was further compounded when, just by chance, Leisha recorded a piece of it 'off the radio'. I now had a 'show reel'. It was a start!

The other highlight that sticks out in my mind was following St Just RFC on their incredible journey in my last season in Cornwall. St Just is a small town, way out west and just before you get to Land's End. Historically this was a mining area and, like most of Cornwall, it's an area of outstanding natural beauty. It has a wonderful atmosphere and it honours its old traditions, such as the 'feast' they hold every November which lasts a few days. This is how the feast was described just over a century ago:

> Rich and poor still at this season keep open house, and all
> the young people from St. Just who are in service for many

miles around, if they can possibly be spared, go home on the Saturday and stay until the Tuesday morning. A small fair is held in the streets on Monday evening, when the young men are expected to treat their sweethearts liberally, and a great deal of 'foolish money' that can be ill afforded is often spent.

Nothing much has changed, except that since 1967 the day also includes a rugby match between St Just and the 'Rucking Feasters XV', an invitational XV selected by the grand old Cornishman, Paul Bawden, who sadly passed away a few years ago. The tradition, however, still continues.

St Just is also unique in that it's the 'first and last' rugby club in England – first if you're approaching from the sea, and last if you're on land. It's a 'junior club' that would often benefit from players nearing the end of their careers at other larger local clubs. St Just play at Tregeseal, a lovely little valley just outside the town. With the advent of the pro era at the Pirates, St Just enjoyed an absolute windfall of talent as virtually their entire first XV had played with the Pirates before the Ringos, Moseleys, Cordles etc. had rocked up in Penzance. Chuck in a few 'Hakes' from St Ives, and St Just went rocketing up through the leagues.

In 1998/99, when I covered them, they reached the semi-final of the John Smith's Vase competition. They were one step away from an appearance at the final in Twickenham. The semi-final was against Billericay in Essex. In an epic encounter, on a sloping pitch, they had a chance to win the game in the last minute, but bombed it and they lost. It was good to see a relatively small club like that achieve so much.

As I said, after a season and a half with Radio Cornwall, I moved to Cardiff to take up my drug rep job, and subsequently buy the Cameo Club. It's here that my previous experience in broadcasting, as little as it was, would become a very useful addition to the banter and conversation with those from the broadcasting world. Opening the club door to the likes of Jonathan Davies, Gwyn Jones, Gareth Charles et al. was certainly a budding commentator's dream. People often think that's how I actually got into broadcasting in the first place, through those that I knew at the club. Hopefully, they now know different.

At the time Gwyn had not long started writing his column for the *Western Mail*. He would often come into the Cameo to rough-cut these pieces. So there was I, sat with an incredible player, chatting about the events of the week in Welsh rugby and the points he might write about. It was great to be there with Gwyn, bouncing ideas off each other, although I hasten to add I take no credit for contributing anything to the actual articles!

I'd been at the Cameo for nearly two years, and got to know lots of BBC staff, including Rhodri Jones, a producer with BBC Sport. At the time there was such a thing as a Welsh Scottish League, when the likes of Edinburgh and Glasgow would play against 12 south Wales clubs. Rhodri mentioned that such a structure gave him a bit of a headache as it meant that there were lots of matches, most of which were played at the same time on a Saturday afternoon, and he struggled to get people to report on them. As he was in full flow, I just said, 'I'd love to do that!' He asked me what I meant by that and I told him of my experiences at Radio Cornwall. I found the tape that Leisha had made of my commentary debut at the Launceston vs St Ives match, and asked him to have a listen.

Later that weekend, myself, Rhod and Gwyn were all gathering at another mate's house, Siôn Thomas. It was at the height of our 'having a good time' era when we spent many an evening together at the Cameo, usually culminating with Siôn insisting on singing songs from *Les Misérables* or *Moulin Rouge* or, worse still, 'Angels' by Robbie Williams, at the top of his voice. On this occasion Rhod said that he'd listened to my tape and 'actually, I wasn't that bad'! Quickly followed by, 'Do you fancy doing Swansea vs Ebbw Vale next weekend?'

So I did. Early September 2001, I turned up at Eugene Cross for my first BBC Wales gig, providing the updates to the main Saturday afternoon sports programme. I remember Ebbw Vale charging down an Arwel Thomas kick to score in the opening minutes. I also recall big Andy Moore, the Wales lock, playing for the Whites and attempting to prevent a long-range Ebbw Vale penalty kick from going over the bar by jumping up to pat the ball away. He didn't succeed, but he did grab the crossbar and swing from it for a few seconds! I don't remember much more about the game to be honest. But it was a start. More broadcast work followed, and I overlapped commentating for the BBC with working at the Cameo. So if you want to blame somebody, blame 'Radio' Rhod Jones! I'm very happy to say that he's still my producer on *Scrum V* on the radio, which goes out at 7.30 p.m. every Thursday on BBC Radio Wales, your home for Welsh sport! Never knowingly undersold... download the podcast!

My break into television came the following season. Geraint Rowlands was an executive producer in the sports department, and he wanted the commentaries that went with the highlights of games on *Scrum V* to be as authentic as possible. He asked those who'd provided updates on games for the radio to provide a 'commentary' for the TV highlights. So if I did an update shift on a Saturday, I'd be back at the BBC the following day to do a voice-over for the try sequence from the game I'd covered.

Also on the Sunday, I became involved in helping Gwyn Jones and Siôn Thomas with their work on the S4C programme, *Y Clwb Rygbi*, which also went out on Sundays, but at lunchtime. Basically, Gwyn would watch all the games and select clips that he wanted to use to make his analysis. Because we were against the clock, and Gwyn needed to move on to the next clip for analysis, I'd then take the clip he'd just analysed to the video truck out at the back of Broadcasting House to ensure that all the arrows and circles that illustrated his points were in the right places.

I learned a great deal about the more technical side of television from doing this work. I also began to appreciate that Gwyn was pretty much unrivalled in his analysis of the game. His application and preparation is simply awesome. A few years ago, while he was having some work done to his house, Gwyn stayed at mine for a while. It was during the Six Nations of 2009, and he would spend five to six hours on his laptop watching games. Logging the salient points, he would then take them to the BBC and spend another five hours or so in an edit suite getting it just right. All that for maybe five minutes of television. It's no wonder that his insight is just about the best in the business. That said, whatever Gwyn does, he does to the best of his abilities, whether it be as a doctor, commentator, analyst, your mate on the pop! I'll never forget his portrayal of Mr Creosote in my 'movie character' themed fancy dress party at my stag do! A far superior effort to Batton and Marty Murrish (one from Cardiff and the other one from Penzance) who coincidentally had the same idea. They both bought a pair of blue overalls and a mask to re-create the character Jason from *Halloween*. As they walked into the bar I can still hear Chad asking them:

'So boys, which movie were the Kwik Fit fitters in?'

Anyway, back to the story. One thing that developed very early on in my work for BBC Wales was including more light-hearted comments in my description of the action. I think that this led to my call-up to appear in front of the camera, something that I never dreamt would happen, blessed as I am with the perfect face for radio! I was asked to pop up for a chat with Geraint Rowlands, as he wanted to discuss plans for the forthcoming season. I want to put something on the record here – these plans had nothing to do with the BBC experimenting in widescreen broadcasting, as Gwyn takes great delight in telling people!

The season in question, 2003/04, was to be the first for the new Welsh regions and it was a World Cup year as well. There was a new buzz word in broadcasting – interactive. It seems that Rowlands thought I might be the man to bring that element into rugby broadcasting. How? By reading e-mails! The aim was to reflect the view of the public in the programme, something which we now think of as second nature in our television programmes. They wanted someone in the studio to read the e-mails that viewers sent in. I had a screen test for the role. John Morgan, a very well-regarded former broadcaster, was asked to give me some advice and guide me through. He was fabulous and helped me a great deal. At one point I was reading from the autocue, and I fluffed a line and made some light-hearted throwaway remark. 'That,' said John, 'was brilliant. You being you really works. Forget trying to be Des Lynam or whoever, just be yourself.' I still probably looked like a rabbit caught in the headlights as I refocused my gaze on the autocue, but John had seen something that he thought could work, and it also gave me something to work on.

The screen test went well enough for me to be trialled in the job. The truth is that in so many aspects of life I don't have that much confidence, and the confident exterior is quite often just a front. I had the confidence to go for the screen test, but I still lacked confidence in my abilities to go through with it. I took a lot of encouragement from the way John handled my training for the screen test and the comments he made to help me along. I also remember him saying, at another time, that if I lost weight I could do most presenting roles. If I wanted to stick to rugby broadcasting, he said, I was OK as I was. But, if I wanted to broaden my horizons... 'Don't take that as a criticism of you,' he said. 'It's just that's how much I believe in you and your abilities.' On a personal level it gave me renewed belief.

So that was me for that rugby season – Rick the trainee autocue reader! I would be in for a good few hours on Sundays, reading through all the e-mails and picking out the best ones and then incorporating them into my script. I'll never forget that first time on *Scrum V*. Graham Thomas was presenting and he was very kind to me. He could easily have seen me as the new boy who was a threat, which is often the case in the media. But he didn't, and he helped me through the first day and that first broadcast in particular. Eddie Butler and Jonathan Davies, the studio guests, were also true pros. I knew Jiffy, of course, from my days in rugby league and the Cameo, and I'd seen Eddie around the sports department of the BBC often. I sat in the studio at a high table, with a laptop in front of me. That slot went well enough from my point of view, but at the end of the season I couldn't disagree with Geraint Rowlands when he said that it needed to be scrapped. There wasn't any real interaction. It didn't really work into the main body of the programme; it was all rather clunky.

Real interaction happens face to face, of course. That was the new plan: to send me out to rugby grounds to talk to fans who'd turned up to watch games. So, on the first Saturday of September 2004, I was posted with producer Steve Jenkins and cameraman Richard Bartley to Oakdale RFC in Gwent. I'm delighted to say that exactly ten years to the day, on the first Saturday of September 2014, I was with the same two boys covering St Davids vs Laugharne!

What's happened to me in the intervening years has been quite remarkable. A three-and-a-half-minute-item on *Scrum V* turned into a ten-year broadcasting career, not to mention the accompanying after-dinner speaking sideline to boot. And, of course, I've got a book out of it too!

The whole idea of going out to grassroots clubs the length and breadth of Wales was certainly the right one. It captured the imagination of an army of loyal rugby fans and players who turn out from Saturday to Saturday, year after year, often in the most difficult circumstances to keep our great game moving forwards. If anyone wants an opinion of the professional game, it's readily available, pre-, during and post-match. What is underrepresented is the amateur game, the production line that feeds the pro game. There's a whole layer of rugby below the professional game which is just as important. Apart from their families, rugby is the most important thing in the lives of thousands of grassroot rugby folk, almost as integral to their being as breathing itself.

What we've tried to do in the items we've made with these people is hold up a mirror to them. Where there's fun to be had, I hope that we've had it; but I really hope that we've never poked fun. We've reflected what rugby is. This is not by being dewy-eyed or romantic in any way. The truth of the matter is that if there weren't over 200 clubs in Wales, we certainly wouldn't have four regions, much less the national side that brings us so much pride.

What makes us go from club to club is great stories,

about individual characters, or a certain significance to a particular fixture. Someone like Tommo was a character; we made a film about him a few years back. He played for Llanishen and we went there to cover his one thousandth game for the club. One thousand games. Unbelievable! On the day that story went out, the studio guest was Warren Gatland. He, of course, had no idea beforehand that we'd be broadcasting that piece during the programme. So, as he watched it being transmitted, he was well impressed with Tommo's feat. After the programme he sent Tommo and his wife a pair of tickets to watch Wales play in one of the following autumn's internationals, plus hospitality. That was a lovely thing to do. Tommo still pulls on his Llanishen shirt; he's now well into his 50s.

A visit to Penallta RFC stays in my mind, too. The club, known as the Pitmen, had come from district level and had fought with the WRU for the right to be recognised as a member club. They established themselves as a union club quite quickly, and flew up through the leagues. They got in touch one day and told me about a special club tradition. After each Saturday game they chose the man of the match, who was then presented with the keys of a Robin Reliant Rialto, the three-wheeler, Del Boy-type vehicle. It was painted in club colours, canary yellow and blue, with 'The Pitmen' written on the sides. That car was the man of the match's vehicle for the following week and he had to drive it everywhere he went! And yes, we did use the *Top Gear* music to accompany the story.

As it turns out we covered Penallta on a few occasions around that time, initially to report on their remarkable success, then the Rialto piece, and finally, if coincidentally, they featured in the Silver Ball final. This proved to be very upsetting to their local rivals, Nelson RFC (the 'Unicorns'), with whom I enjoy a very close relationship, having met Adrian 'Spud the Legend' Withers at their club dinner ten years ago. I will always remember Spud, Chunky, Marshy, Candy, and Farrow taking to the terrace at Sardis Road to unfurl a banner demanding equal rights from *Scrum V* for Nelson RFC. Great fun from a great bunch of boys who, to me, epitomise what grassroots rugby is all about, and although I'm friendly with this pack, my experience tells me that every club in Wales has a similar core support that live and breathe for their club and community.

Just as in life itself, some of the best stories unfold by accident. Trebanos against Maesteg Celtic was one such story. The bus driver got lost on the way there, and we were filming the whole lot! We got to a point where we could see the clubhouse and the pitch, but we couldn't get round to it. In the end, the team got off and ran through this woman's garden (with her permission), over hedges, across the railway line and onto the pitch. As it happened – grassroots rugby!

Sometimes, it's a milestone in the rich heritage of Welsh rugby that leads the story. Such an occasion was filming the centenary fixture between Llandovery College and Christ's College, Brecon. That particular fixture has a very special tradition and it was an honour to be there that day. It's the ultimate achievement in the school rugby career of every one of those boys on the pitch. Certain traditions have been attached to that game over the years and are religiously observed. For example, no one is allowed to set foot in any way on the first XV's pitch unless they've played in the match against Brecon. The players chosen are presented with their socks the night before the match, and they have to wear them to bed. There's a service in the chapel on the morning of the match; then the entire school gather in the hall and the players chosen have to run the gauntlet of their school mates to rapturous applause. The players collect their jerseys and go straight to the dressing rooms.

When they run out onto the pitch, they have to touch a toy monkey which they pass on their way. It's a definite, time-honoured ritual, steeped in tradition, observed by hundreds of boys over the century, including internationals such as Gwyn Jones, Alun Wyn Jones, Craig Quinnell, Peter Rogers and George North. Unlike Gwyn and George, that fixture can be the pinnacle of their rugby career. Most won't go on to play for a first-class team or their country, so they hold that match in very high regard and look back at their time on the pitch that day with great pride.

Unfortunately, that fixture is no longer. It was brought to an end following concerns regarding health and safety. Llandovery has become a centre of rugby excellence, while the college at Brecon has dedicated itself to more academic pursuits. Results were becoming increasing lopsided, so the fixture was no longer viable. The 'old boys' of both colleges, however, were not having that. They've picked up the gauntlet and started an old boys' fixture between the two colleges in order to keep the tradition going. That is just typical of rugby boys; they would not allow all that history and culture to go quietly into that good night.

Sometimes the stories are just plain bonkers! One such story seems to have captured the imagination of the rugby-loving public; it involved me dressing up as a pig! I'd been asked by *Scrum V* producer Craig Withycome to interview Kees Meeuws, the All Black prop. He'd just signed for the Scarlets and they wanted me to have a word with him about his move to Wales. I was chuffed with that for two reasons; firstly, because they normally send a proper journalist to record such items and secondly, the chance to interview a world-class prop like Kees was just a dream. Craig had added, somewhat sheepishly, that Kees' hobby back home in New Zealand was hunting wild boar. 'OK,' I said, interested in the fact, but unable to see its relevance to my interview. Until they said, 'Well, what we were kind of hoping was that you might possibly dress up as a pig and let him hunt you at the paintballing centre after the interview.' Craig was very tentative with this request. 'Yes, OK, no problem,' I said back.

Craig seemed taken aback by my instant willingness to be subjected to such treatment. From my point of view, the experience would allow me to talk to Kees Meeuws and I would do anything for that to happen. When I see Kees these days, he comes over to say hello and we end up having a beer. That's worth dressing up as a pig for.

The cameraman with me that day was, once again, 'Barters' Bartley. He admitted later that he actually got the 'money shot' of Kees shooting me in the arse on the very first take, but that he sent me back out another three or four times again because he really enjoyed watching me get shot in the arse by an All Black prop! That's another aspect of filming, the fun that we have as a crew. We have a motto, 'We don't go far but we have some fun!'

I've had some great fun, but the items have been successful because of the talent of the people that I've worked with; they're simply the best the BBC has to offer. After ten years this list is a long one, but I must mention a few and hope that those omitted are not too upset. All of the items are beautifully shot because the cameramen are superb: Barters, Mark 'Corporal' Thorne and 'Chicken' Jeff Thomas. These guys are used on the Six Nations network coverage, and bring you the very tight close-up shots of the action which are then used in the beautiful video packages in previews of the games. I remember one item we filmed at

Senghenydd on a dark and dreary afternoon. It was produced by Laura Nicklin. Barters captured the moment at the final whistle just as the players shook hands; they appeared like silhouettes, dark grey against light grey mist and drizzle. It was truly magical; the whole thing looked like a Kyffin Williams masterpiece that had come to life.

The producers that I've worked with have also been sensational and all have a very different style. Steve Jenkins, the poor sod that had to take me on originally, really understands rugby. He used to play for Taff's Well. He knows exactly who the characters are and how to edit the pieces to really convey the greatness of the grassroots game. David Purchase, on the other hand, knows very little about the game on a technical level, but has a great sense of drama and spectacle and is extremely creative; some of his items are almost like mini Hollywood movies. Tariq Ali has a wicked sense of humour and it was his idea to get me emerging from the surf at Langland Bay, à la Daniel Craig. Tal, Chris Howells, Rhys Edwards, even Siôn Thomas himself, have joined my odyssey around Wales and beyond. This brings us to Ceri Jenkins. He's a young buck, a right little chancer from west Wales with whom I've had a load of fun working on those Six Nations items, scouting Wales' opponents and adopting England! Just me, him, a hand-held digital camera, and a massive appetite for adventure! Rome in the snow!

The progression for me was going from reading e-mails to filming in clubs all over Wales, and then also working on the 'red button'. This latter step up came from a need to develop alternative types of commentary to enhance the experience of the rugby television viewer. There was always going to be the main match commentary. We also now had the coaches'/officials' option, when you could choose to listen to coaches and referees, such as Derek Bevan and Tony

Clement, discussing the finer technical points of the game. The Welsh-language option on the red button gave those who wanted to listen to the match in Welsh that particular choice. My brief on the red button, again from Rowlands, was to try to bring the terraces – the banter and jollity that you get standing out in the cold with a pint in your hand – to the comfort of sofa viewing. That would happen by way of my interviewing a fan from each team and having a rugby terrace type conversation on the microphone. If there was a lull in play, we'd talk about all sorts of things related to rugby, not necessarily linked to the game we were watching – exactly as you would do if you went to see a game live. Over the years, these fans have become broadcasting stalwarts in their regions, and the more biased they are, the better the programme!

One lady, Jeannie Harris, a Yorkshire lass, picked up on this red button commentary and started to follow us from week to week. While listening, she learned that my dad had gone to Lewis School, Pengam, where her husband had also been a pupil, but after my dad's schooldays. Some time later her husband sadly died after a brief illness. When she heard that I was going to medical school, she sent me the stethoscope which I now wear every single day when I'm at work. She had it engraved with 'Rick O'Shea' and she also added the motto of Lewis School, Pengam, 'Ni Ddychwel Ddoe', meaning 'Yesterday Never Returns'. That's quite a special gesture.

The red button facility started slowly enough. It was not everybody's cup of tea, and I can imagine that it must have been quite annoying to those outside Wales for whom it was the only option available! It gathered momentum as fans throughout Britain realised that they could pick this up. Even if they couldn't get Jiffy and Charlo (Gareth Charles) they still stuck around, or possibly turned the volume down! The audience was encouraged to text the show and take part in discussions. At the height of the service we would get an average of about 400 texts for a standard club game. Our record was 800 texts, during a Wales vs Fiji game.

The interesting thing about all this television experience is that I always wanted to be a commentator. I would still love to commentate more regularly. Luckily, I've had a few opportunities to do so, not only with the Beeb, but I've done a few Heineken Cup games for Sky, too. Commentating is a real craft. You only have to listen to a bad one to appreciate that. At the moment I'm a bad commentator who wants to be a good one. It's a difficult and often lonely position to occupy. You only have to look at Eddie Butler to see that. The English hate him because they think he's pro-Welsh, and half the Welsh hate him because they think he's pro-English. Eddie, in the meantime, carries on with his work, not overly concerned about what anyone thinks. In my view there really is no finer wordsmith than Eddie. He's doing more and more non rugby programmes now, and I think it's great for features and documentaries to benefit from the colour that he brings to a story.

I also happen to have had a great piece of advice from Eddie, the one I mentioned briefly in the opening chapter. I've had really good advice from many, some of whom you've read about in this chapter. But Eddie told me once, when I'd asked him to look over an article I'd written for *Red Handed* magazine, 'Rick, my dear boy, it reads well. But my opinion shouldn't matter. All I would say to you is this, be loved, be hated but never be ignored.' I can work with that.

15

AND THEN THERE'S the Six Nations, of course! Back to where we began this tale. *Scrum V*'s live Six Nations format varied significantly from the week in, week out programme, and it offered me personally another type of opportunity. BBC Wales Six Nations *Scrum V* now comes live from the BBC Club. It was initially presented by Jason Mohammad; now Ross Harries has taken up the reins. It has proven to be a very popular format, which was well thought-out by the BBC. Well, actually that might not be entirely true. It all started during the 2007 World Cup, the one we didn't do particularly well in.

ITV had the broadcast rights for that particular tournament and, as a result, the BBC didn't have any access to footage. The previous World Cup was in New Zealand, with matches broadcast at ungodly hours. In 2007, however, the competition was in France, with very little time difference between us and them. Match kick-offs were at times which were very convenient for Welsh viewers, and that made things worse. It was unthinkable that *Scrum V* would be off-air during the World Cup, even if there was no match footage. But to make things worse, Gareth Lewis, *Scrum V*'s front man at that time, was out in France as the programme's rugby correspondent, with Gareth Charles. So a new format and a new presenter was needed.

Someone had the idea of doing a live programme from the BBC Club in Llandaf. So the format was sorted. But who to present it? Jason was asked to do it, and he excelled. The original idea was borne out of a pragmatic response to a situation the BBC inherited, and it's just carried on like that ever since.

The actual programme created for the 2007 World Cup, which had all the makings of a hospital pass when it was thrown our way, suddenly took off and became a huge hit with the audience. A lot of that was down to the fact that many people raised on the BBC's rugby coverage have struggled to take to ITV's coverage, not because of the quality of their production per se, but because of all the commercial breaks interrupting the analysis.

That run of *Scrum V* definitely proved one thing: if you can get the right people to talk about rugby in front of a live audience, it will work. There was no shortage of great players we could call upon of course, including All Black Justin Marshall, Phil Bennett, Gwyn Jones and Ryan Jones (who couldn't play in that World Cup because of injury). It was also the last time I saw Grav. What a man Ray Gravell was. I couldn't possibly do him justice in a few lines, but I will say this – no matter where or when you met him you always felt better after seeing him. Over a pint after the programme, I apologised for not being able to go and see him when he was in hospital.

'It doesn't matter, bach' he said with his usual passion. 'I'm seeing you now!'

My role on that new *Scrum V* was to do live chats with various groups who were in the audience. I was the link between the audience and the panel. Jason would hand over to me every so often and I would ask people who were there from different rugby clubs what they thought about the things the panel was discussing. The whole format proved so successful that it was brought back for the following Six Nations, where it has stayed ever since. I did the World Cup, and the following Six Nations series in 2008 and 2009, before Dot Davies and Lisa Rogers brought a much-needed ladies' touch.

The work I was doing for the BBC was increasing and I was becoming an established part of their rugby coverage. This had a very unexpected side effect, which I saw very clearly one day at a cricket match!

Gwyn Jones rang me up to say that he had some tickets for the Cardiff Ashes Test match; would I like to join him for the second day? That was a definite yes then! We met at the Cameo for breakfast first, which might even have included a pint. We walked down to Sophia Gardens and took our seats, right up in the gods, as it happened, next to Jim Rosenthal. When we'd finished our drinks we clearly needed to get more, which we did during an interval in play. That meant going back down loads of steps to fetch them but the thought of climbing all the way back up to our seats was a little daunting. The stewards nearby sensed what was going through our minds, and told us that many people didn't return to their seats after the lunch interval, so they were happy to keep us some seats further down to save us going back up to the gods again.

We were very grateful for that, and hung around the concourse for a while, with the match restarting after the drinks interval. We bumped into Chad, and Neil 'Lofty' Watkins, a second row who had toured North America with Wales when Gwyn was captain. He didn't play for Llanishen, but he was an honorary 'Chimp' and central to many of those unprintable stories! We also chanced upon Brian Howells, who used to work for a drinks' wholesaler that supplied the Cameo, and he invited us along to the Wolf Blass tent. It wasn't a tent really, more of a posh shed with a bar in it. Whatever it was, that's where we stayed for the rest of the game. I have no idea if those stewards kept the seats for us, but if they did, thank you, and sorry we didn't turn up!

Come about teatime, I bumped into Steve James, the former Glamorgan batsman and then, as now, a writer for the *Telegraph*. He is a great bloke and I yelled across to him, ever so slightly the worse for wear, 'Hey Jamer, I hope you put it in your article tomorrow... Tell them Jamer... that Cardiff is the cricketing capital of the world! Look at it! Look at it!' He duly humoured me with some suitable put down and moved on.

We were pretty 'tired and emotional' by now. Gwyn went to the toilet and fell asleep in there; we didn't see him for another couple of hours. I'd been used to drinking obviously, but had fallen out of the habit a little in the months preceding this Test match as by now I was at medical school. Added to that, it was wine we'd been hitting, not pints – as was more usually the case. I remember several attempts at trying to rise from my chair to stand up, but failing miserably. I wobbled significantly and my legs were obviously not working. As stumps were nearing, the stewards nearby witnessed my several attempts to stand on my own two feet and realised that it was never going to happen. They summoned a golf buggy and put me and those I was with in it. They drove us to the Daffodil Gates at the entrance of the cricket ground and dumped us outside.

I stumbled off the back off the buggy and tripped into a hedge. There was enough blood on my forehead to warrant the attention of the St John Ambulance people. They put me on a stretcher and took me to their tent. While I was there, Gwyn came in and said, 'I'm a doctor, there's nothing wrong with him, he's coming with me!' And out we went.

Everybody was leaving the ground now, so hundreds of people were thronging round us. The boys managed to get a taxi to take me home, and dumped me on the doorstep where Leisha was extremely surprised at the state I was in, having never seen me like this before. She ordered a pizza, because I hadn't eaten since breakfast, I know... she's a keeper. I ate it and crashed out.

The next morning wasn't good. To say I felt awful would be an understatement. In the middle of that hangover mist and fog, I received an e-mail from Geoff Williams, the head of BBC Wales Sport. He wanted to have a chat with me and told me to contact him as soon as I could. I rang him immediately.

'Hi Geoff, I just got your message, how can I help you?'

'I need to have a chat with you.'

'I'm OK to talk now.'

'No, that's not OK, can you come up to the BBC for a chat please? We need to talk face to face.'

That did not sound good. I made my way to Llandaf with all sorts of questions whirling round in my head. The main one was, what on earth had actually happened yesterday and did I do something that I can't remember doing? I walked into the sports department and could sense the chuckles and guffaws of my colleagues as I walked past them, before things fell to a deathly silence as I neared the door of Geoff's office.

'What on the earth happened to you yesterday?' was his first question to me.

So it definitely was about yesterday then, I thought to myself. Before I could put an answer together, he carried on.

'I've been out with you after a match for a few beers and you're always very good at handling your drink and in the way you behave.'

'I am usually,' I replied, 'but I haven't been out much

recently and maybe I'm not as good as I thought I was and certainly not as good as I used to be. I mixed wine and beer, which is never any good, and I suppose I just went for it. But I obviously couldn't handle it.'

'OK,' said Geoff, 'yesterday wasn't good. You must remember, whether you like it or not, people will recognise you, especially in the sporting circles of south Wales. I'm not saying that you have to be squeaky clean whenever you go out, but Rick, you were at one of the most high-profile events in Wales, in any sport, ever! You must be aware that you have a responsibility, not only to yourself, but to *Scrum V* and the BBC as well. You let yourself and us down yesterday.'

I apologised unreservedly, fearing the worst.

'However,' Geoff continued, 'putting things in a broader context of knowing you as I do, and knowing how you usually are, I will treat this as an aberration. I will take a different view if you do it again, however.'

I apologised sincerely and thanked him for the way he'd dealt with it. I emphasised that I did feel it a real privilege to work for the BBC and that I wouldn't let them down again. As I was ready to leave, I had to ask one more question. How did he know what happened the day before?

'How did I know about it? How did I know? By about six o'clock I'd had a text message from the head of sport at ITV, a text message from the head steward at Glamorgan Cricket Club, and there were a load of messages and photos on Twitter. And if that wasn't enough, as Wyre Davies was setting up for his piece to camera for *Wales Today*, you were seen in the back of the shot being taken on a stretcher to the St John Ambulance tent!'

There was no arguing with that! It doesn't get much more obvious than being seen carried on a stretcher on a television news item made by the company I work for. The whole thing did teach me a hell of a lot about what it means to be in the public eye, whatever your level of TV exposure.

At the beginning of the 2013/14 season, the red button service that I'd been hosting was moved to radio. By now, the service had evolved into a more considered discussion, featuring ex-players, most often the excellent Gareth Llewellyn, known simply as the 'Master' and, increasingly, Paul Williams, an uncommonly well-informed and equally bizarrely dressed chap from Gowerton. Apparently, he was once voted the eighth best dressed man in Wales by the *Western Mail* he says – I think it was more likely his mum!

This coincided with changes in the broader sporting landscape in Wales. We now had two football teams in the Premiership, as Cardiff had just secured promotion to the top flight, joining Swansea. It was felt that this would increase the need for sporting discussion and analysis across more than one sport. As a result, Radio Wales' schedule was revamped to include a Monday to Friday 7 p.m. to 9 p.m. sports slot. I was invited to present a two-hour programme on Friday nights. I wasn't sure at first whether any rugby input would be hugely successful on a night when the BBC itself was also broadcasting live rugby on television, but the programmes still proved popular. So much so, that the programme was moved to Thursday nights from the start of the current 2014/15 season.

We couldn't have got off to a better start. The very first programme of this run, 28 August, was, coincidentally, the day when the Welsh Rugby Union and Regional Rugby Wales announced their long-awaited peace deal. My studio guests that night were Martyn Williams, Jonathan Davies and Paul Williams. We had a full programme sorted, which included analysis of what we could expect in the forthcoming season of the PRO 12 and Aviva Premiership rugby championships. We managed to get Sean Holley onto the programme by about 8.55 p.m., and once again I crashed into the top of the *Chris Needs* show! The whole of the previous hour and a half or so had been taken up with just the one story – the peace deal. Again, proof if it ever were needed that if you get people together to talk about Welsh rugby, you can fill hours of broadcasting.

The studio guests contributed to that, of course. Jiffy got us off to a good start, I must say. He quoted Roger Lewis as saying that during the negotiations for the deal there had been no crossed words between the union and the regions. Jiffy's response to that was, quite simply, 'Well, that's a lie!' Nothing like a definite statement to generate a response! Martyn Williams said that the deal sounded good, but he had concerns over the practicalities of how it was going to work – a point reiterated the following week when Gareth 'Alfie' Thomas came on the show.

So the programme was evolving as we went along, in order to react to the public who were contacting us to discuss really important issues in Welsh rugby. The same kind of thing had happened in the previous series, when the programme was on a Friday night, and on a related issue. We'd invited David Moffett to the studio on the day he'd launched his manifesto in his bid to be elected to the board of the WRU. We also invited the WRU to send someone to discuss the proposals with David Moffett, but they declined. So we had a discussion with Moffett alone. I've mentioned Moffett's fight with the WRU many a time on the programme. The BBC received a fair degree of criticism during the coverage of this particular episode from some quarters, feeling that we hadn't given Moffett's view a fair hearing. Whenever I hear that point or, as is more likely, read it in a 'tweet' or a post on a message board, I just say simply that Moffett was my studio guest for over an hour and twenty minutes. He didn't get a free run, however. Gareth Lewis ensured that he was editorially scrutinized.

As previously stated, I may be best suited to radio aesthetically, but I also love it as a medium as it gives you a scope that TV can't often offer. Hosting *Scrum V* on the radio was also going some way towards minimising the one thing that I feared about my TV work – perhaps some people regarded me as a bit of a clown. It's not a massive issue. I suppose that agreeing to dress up as a pig and be shot at in the backside doesn't help that image! I do have a lot of fun on the radio as well, of course. But at least on my radio programme, I'm addressing the important issues and asking serious questions.

For example, there's still a question I would like an answer to. It's related to the Moffett/WRU issue we've already alluded to. About 40 clubs thought it necessary to call for an EGM of the WRU to discuss the perceived crisis in the Welsh game. But, when that meeting was held, only two or three clubs showed any opposition. What had happened to the rest? Did they all change their minds and move from concern to support in a matter of weeks? Why haven't we been told why they changed their minds? People in Wales don't normally climb down in such a way. Maybe I'll get the chance to ask the question one day, and maybe I'll get an answer. It's fascinating that just weeks later, WRU chairman Dai Pickering was voted out as a national representative by grassroots clubs in a surprise outcome, with ex-Welsh internationals Anthony Buchanan and Gareth Davies getting seats on the 18-strong board, with Gareth Davies subsequently elected as the WRU's new chairman.

You can't ignore politics in Welsh rugby. The task for me

is to make sure that I don't get embroiled in the political process and the heat it generates. I need to try to be aware of the way these political decisions affect the grassroots fans. That means reading the barometer of their opinion in any way I can. I do browse various related websites; *Gwlad*, in particular, is a very good research tool. It's populated by many passionate and well-informed people. The problem is that it's a web forum, and most 'posters' do so anonymously and, as such, normal rules of etiquette and social interaction do not apply. It's often not long before the toys come out of the pram and the debate gets personal. The truth is, however, that I also visit enough rugby clubs and meet enough people to keep on top of the way these people who prop up the game feel about it. Because, for them as well, it's all rugby, isn't it?

16

You MIGHT WELL have picked up a theme running between the sentences and paragraphs of this book. There have been many times when I've felt that I've underachieved. That's been true at school, in college, as a rep, in broadcasting, and of course, in rugby. When I left the Cameo there was a very strong sense of underachieving and also a definite lack of direction. I'd walked away from the club and bought a restaurant in Cornwall. But that was really meant to be an investment.

Throughout most of my Cameo days, Leisha had been employed as a nanny with a lovely and very wealthy family in London, an incredible position that put her very firmly at the summit of her profession. Sadly, as is the nature of that work, the children grew up and the job came to an end. With the CV and references she now possessed, she was very quickly picked up by another family in London, but I think that the job she'd held for five years could not be topped, and working in London was losing its appeal, too. I had my occasional BBC work, but that hadn't escalated to the level you've just read about, at that time. The broadcasting work I had at the time wouldn't sustain us. Basically, I needed a job.

There was only one thing for it. I had to go back to repping. I went back to the old familiar places to see if there were any jobs around, and another dear old pal, Gethin Evans, took a chance on me, offering me a locum post to cover one of his reps who was away on maternity leave. When the locum work was up, I'd done enough to impress the management at Sanofi-Aventis to earn a full-time post in another division, under a chap named Amal Luchmun. I was to sell Lantus, a relatively new insulin analogue that proved to be a game changer, not only in the world of endocrinology but also in mine.

Amal, like Gethin, was a great manager, and he encouraged me to get involved with not only promoting the product but also better understanding the management of diabetes in general. This now brings us back to the Cameo Club once again. One of the members was a consultant endocrinologist called Marc Evans. I got in touch with him and asked if I could chat with him about clinical management so that I could learn more about diabetes. It paid off, and through this increased knowledge I was better placed when discussing with GPs the role of the product and the patients who might benefit most. I did really well with this product, eventually becoming national sales champion.

My brief was simple. Insulin had traditionally been the preserve of experts in hospitals. However, as Type II diabetes was becoming more prevalent, GPs needed to take a more active role in its management. A part of my job was to help up-skill GPs to do just that. Each GP has on average 2,500 patients. It's estimated, probably conservatively, that about six per cent of the population has diabetes. So there will be a few hundred diabetics on any GP's list. Broadly speaking, each GP would react to this offer in one of two ways: either, they recognised the growing problem posed by diabetes and got onboard, or they saw the need but were too busy at that particular time to come to the training courses, but would consider doing so in the future.

A small minority would offer a third opinion: 'It's not my job, that's what diabetes units in hospitals should be doing, not GPs'! I remember one GP in particular, who I won't name, being particularly arrogant about his attitude to treating people with diabetes. He wound me up so much that I remember thinking, as I sat opposite him, 'F*** you! I'm going to go to medical school. I'm going to train to be a doctor. I'm going to be a GP who will specialise in the treatment of diabetes. The few hundred diabetics on my list would get the best treatment they could.'

This was thought out a little more rationally during a conversation with Gwyn Jones and Marc Evans at the Cameo, as we sat in the IKEA bucket chairs that I'd personally bought from the store in Bristol. I told Gwyn and Marc that a colleague of mine at Sanofi, Andy Davies, had just got on to the graduate entry course for Medicine at Swansea University. I was proud of Andy for that achievement, as it showed that the drug rep was capable of far more than just carrying a bag. I also told my two friends that my overriding emotion concerning this was one of envy. I was jealous of Andy for making such a step, and for transforming his life in that way. They both said pretty much the same thing, 'If you feel like that O'Shea, why don't you do it?'

I was 38 years old. That was one of my objections to their idea. Gwyn was having none of it. 'OK, you've missed the entry for this year, but if you get on next year, you'll qualify when you're 44. You'll probably work until you're 70, so that's 25, 26 years of practise. That's more than enough for anyone.'

I can't afford it. That was my next objection. Yes you can, came the reply, reminding me that I had property and a business in Mousehole. Leisha had a good job. I had my broadcasting work and after dinner-speaking engagements. I was in much better shape that your average 18 year old setting off on an undergraduate course.

OK then, I played my final trump card.

I didn't have the marbles for it. Gwyn was ready with his answer again. 'Well sit the entrance exam, and that will soon tell you if you've got what it takes.'

And, as was so often the case, I'd been outmanoeuvered by Gwyn.

So, I went to find out what I needed to get on the course. I needed a 2.1 or better in my previous degree. That was OK.

I needed to sit the GAMSAT exam which, according to Andy, was always held in January.

It's a three-stage paper. The first one is similar to old-fashioned intelligence tests, where you're asked to show your reasoning powers and deal with probabilities and pattern recognition in various scenarios. The second paper was right up my street. We had to write two essays in an hour on subjects they gave us. The third paper is the biggest one. It's called Reasoning in Physical Sciences and consists of 200 questions. We had to show that we knew a bit of Biology, a bit of Chemistry, a bit of Maths, and a bit of Physics. I think that, if my memory serves me correctly, in order to pass the GAMSAT exam, you were required to pass all three papers, and could not score less than 55 per cent in any two of them. I may however be wrong. Whatever the requirements, it was a tough exam.

As stated, I thought the exam was to be held in January. I applied at the end of August only to discover that they'd brought the exam forward to 21 September, so not five months later as I thought. And I read that on August bank holiday! I had a few weeks to prepare! I took all the annual leave that was due to me and started to swot like mad. I crammed every bit of knowledge I could, I practised writing to set times, I tried past papers. It was intense. I also spoke to some who had tried the exam.

I'd bought an online guide to sitting GAMSAT. It stated that there would be times, most definitely, when I would have to guess an answer. The advice of the author on such occasions was to guess consistently. He said that I should always guess using the same letter answer. For example, if I guessed answer 'b' in one question, the next guess should be answer 'b' as well. 'If you think about it logically,' he said, 'if you jump around all the possible letters, you're more likely to miss over the course of the whole paper. Stick to the same guess and you're more likely to hit the right one more often.' A monkey could get 25 per cent using this method, and he went on to say that in his experience of the paper I was trying, they were usually weighted to answers 'b' and 'c'. Again, sound advice for me at a crucial time, even if I was a little more uncertain about the authenticity of these particular words as I went to sit my exam.

Come the day, it was very intense. We started at nine with paper one, and that finished at midday. Then, an hour off for lunch, before sitting paper two which lasted an hour. There was another break, then the third paper for three hours. I had 60 per cent for the first paper, so one pass. In the essay paper I had over 80 per cent. One of the topics given was, 'Patriotism is the last refuge of the scoundrel: discuss'! The third paper was a killer. I decided to guess answer 'c' in any question I wasn't sure of. I don't know how that affected my end result, but I got 51 per cent in it. I was twice as bright as a monkey and I'd just scraped through! LFB!

I'd passed the much vaunted GAMSAT and, in so doing, saw my last barrier to applying for medical school evaporate. I had, it would appear, enough marbles to move on to the next stage. Gwyn was very quick to point out that I'd now run out of excuses!

I was granted an interview and have never been more

nervous in my life than when I was walking to the interview for a place on that degree course. That was because, by then, I really, really wanted it. One of the panel of two recognised me from my TV work, and soon brought that into the questioning.

'How will you manage your broadcasting commitments when you're working nights the day before?'

'You're 40 now, how will you cope with the demands of medical school and then ward life if you qualify, combined with weekend broadcasting and all the stress and travel that comes with it?'

'This isn't really for you, is it?'

'I've worked in my own business,' I replied and related the story of the Cameo. If I'd succeeded in working there under the conditions I had, then I could take anything my new world was going to throw at me.

'I've worked from eight in the morning to three or four the following day,' I said.

'Are you comparing medicine to running a pub?' was the immediate response.

I wasn't, of course, and I reassured them of that. I was just qualifying my reply, intending to show that I wasn't afraid of hard work. I left the room downhearted. It hadn't gone well. We were told the date on which we'd be informed if we'd succeeded or not, and that we'd be told either way. That day came. But there was no letter saying either yes or no for me at my home. I've always been impatient. I decided to phone the medical school and ask what the situation was. I explained that I hadn't received a letter. The woman who answered the phone told me not to worry. But I was worried that I hadn't received a letter; I needed to know like everyone else! 'No, no,' she said, 'don't worry about the letter. You're in. I posted your offer myself, yesterday. Congratulations!'

I was driving through Ely in my company car, a Lexus, at the time, and I was overjoyed, as the rest of Ely probably gathered!

In September 2008 I was to start my training as a doctor. I'd finally been selected, and the day had arrived when I could begin to show my big match potential.

17

I WAS GOING to be a student again! Swansea University's College of Medicine was formed in 2004 as part of a strategic initiative between the Welsh Government and Swansea University to reduce the shortfall in the number of qualified doctors working in Wales. This was a four-year course instead of the usual five or, in some cases, six, undertaken in conventional undergraduate courses. That meant the academic calendar was in the region of 40 weeks, a fair bit longer than a standard degree. But, not only that, it was also pretty much a Monday to Friday, nine to five, series of lectures and practical sessions.

The night before my first day 'at school', I thought that it was important to immerse myself in the world of medicine, so I stayed with Dr Gwyn Jones at his parents' home in Loughor, near Swansea. His mum and dad, Esyllt and Alfie, are also doctors, and so I felt this set a very good tone. In no way did I see it as an opportunity for myself and Gwyn to join Andy Davies (who was about to start his second year) and a few freshers – that I'd come into contact with through Facebook – to hit Wind Street! I felt it had to be done in the interests of social integration, you understand.

This did not however set the tone for my time at Medical School. In truth, it was totally different to being a student the first time round, mainly because I was actually studying, and I hardly ever went out on the pop. Despite this, I made new friends. At 9 a.m. on day one, I met Taymour Sahami from Carmarthen, and John Lambley from Pontardawe, and we were never separated. They became my friends all the way through to the finals and beyond. We sat in the back row, of course, alongside Julia Kramer and Amy Calo. In front of us was a sizeable delegation of Irish guys, Connor Moran, and the splendidly named Ryan O'Neal, alongside Ian Lavelle, a Leinster fan who once joined me on the red button for a game against the Ospreys, Barry Quinn and Niall Killeen. Needless to say, these long-lost cousins became pretty close friends, too.

I was not only challenged academically; the logistics were quite a test also. For most of the first year, I caught a bus to Swansea from Cardiff. I would cycle from my home in Pontcanna to Leckwith, throw my bike in the boot of the bus, and then cycle from the bus station in Swansea along the magnificent seafront past St Helen's to the university. In the second year the timetable became a bit less hectic, so I would drive a bit more often, in a 20-year-old Mondeo that Marc had loaned me since I'd given the Lexus back to Sanofi! I would often give Connor a lift and it was during these journeys that he effectively tutored me through some of the more difficult aspects of physiology, such as acid base balance, the clotting cascade and how kidneys work. Actually, scrap the last one, I'm still not convinced that I entirely understand how kidneys work, but the important thing is that I know how to spot when they are not working!

It was a relentless experience. Probably tougher than I now let on, or even remember. The graduate entry course, like undergraduate medicine, is split into two stages. Pre-clinical training, effectively lecture and lab-based learning, followed by clinical training which is more ward-based. The big difference with the graduate entry was that your pre-clinical training – which is usually three years as an undergraduate – was squeezed into two years. The course at Swansea was excellent – I would say that, I guess – but it really was. There was an emphasis on delivering clinical skills from day one, and the team that taught us was superb. They ensured that we were comfortable and competent in taking a good history, that we understood the components of the physical examination, and then at formulating subsequent management plans.

It was, however, demanding. It was modular in that we would tackle the anatomy and physiology of the major systems of the body individually: gastroenterology, musculoskeletal, cardiology, respiratory etc. The first year was a constant cycle of completing modules, followed by exams every three months or so, at Christmas, Easter and in the summer. If you failed a module you could resit that paper again once in the summer. If you failed again you'd be put back a year, or, if your failure was epic enough, you'd be asked to leave. The second year repeated the cycle of modules, but focused on the pathophysiology of the systems, effectively how they can go wrong and the therapies that were indicated. There were no longer exams every three months; instead we sat a massive 'wheat from chaff' block of exams, called the intermediates, at Easter. Twelve exams in ten days. As I'm writing this I'm becoming more impressed with myself!

I failed only one paper in the two years of pre-clinical training, Health in Society, which I sat during the summer block of the first year. This module was heavy in statistics and also contained aspects of philosophy and sociology, and I basically thought that I could bluster my way through it. So I dedicated more revision time to neurology and endocrinology instead. Big mistake! But with only one exam to resit in the summer, I didn't repeat that error!

And so I made it through to the clinical training for which we joined the fourth-year students at Cardiff Medical School in placements throughout south Wales. The intention there was that you'd observe doctors and nurses at close range and take as many opportunities as you could to roll up your sleeves (not only metaphorically speaking but also from an infection control point of view! That will earn me brownie points with the ward sister!) and get hands-on. I really enjoyed my clinical training; the pace of learning was less intense, but no less vital. It also put you in situations that make for great anecdotes, such as this:

During my block in paediatrics, I'd taken the opportunity to work a night shift. There was only myself and a registrar on-call. In the early hours we were called to the delivery suite to attend a birth, and just after the registrar had performed the standard checks in an adjoining room, dad popped his head around the door.

'Is it a boy or a girl?' he asked.

I helped the registrar wrap a little blanket around the baby.

'Congratulations, you have a beautiful baby girl,' I said.

Dad seemed a little distracted.

'Are you Rick O'Shea?' he enquired.

'Yes,' I replied.

'Oh my god, I love *Scrum V*,' he said and opened the door to shout to his wife. 'Guess who's in here, love?'

At this point I doubt George Clooney would have been of any interest to her, let alone Fatty off *Scrum V*!

'I can't believe it, you've made my day!' he added.

'Made your day? Are you joking! Here's your daughter. Go and share the moment with mum!'

He was a lovely chap and we had a good chat the next day on the ward round. I've learned to never underestimate what three and a half minutes on *Scrum V* can do!

There were, of course, continuous assessments during

these placements of competence and efficiency in core clinical skills, and also a set of exams at the end of the year. Momentum was gradually building towards the sharp end: March 2012 and 'finals'. I too sat my finals in the middle of the Six Nations, just like my friend and colleague Dr Jamie Roberts, although it has to be said to far less acclaim! After all, I was working for *Scrum V* and not playing for Wales.

Curiously enough the night before the results were released I was, perhaps ironically, with Jamie and Nigel Owens, another Welsh legend I'm proud to call a friend, at the Hi Tide in Porthcawl. We were in the middle of the first run of Q&A evenings sponsored by the brewers Molson Coors, ones that have become a regular series of evenings that punctuate the Six Nations and autumn series matches. Jamie knew that I'd get my results the following day, and suggested that we went for a drink to settle my nerves. By the time we'd finished the gig and were back in Cardiff, we couldn't find anywhere open; even the Cameo was shut! It was agreed that we'd meet up for a couple of pints the following night instead, and I went home to try and sleep.

I will never ever forget the following morning. Medicine is a pass or fail course, it's that simple and that brutal. In the old days a 'pass list' was posted on the School notice board, in a very public place. An almighty scrum would ensue as students scanned the sheets, with the vast majority reeling away as doctors. And a desolated few as failures. These days the Deanery is a little more sensitive. A list, not of names, but anonymous university numbers, is e-mailed to you. If your number is on the list you have passed.

I opened the e-mail. There were over 300 numbers on

the list and the Swansea students were always at the end. I scrolled up and down, down and up, looking for my number. Then Leisha looked. My number wasn't there. Jamie texted me to ask how things had gone.

'I didn't make the cut,' was my downbeat reply.

I subsequently received a further e-mail about two hours later, breaking down my performance and explaining what had happened. I'd passed the written papers that assess clinical knowledge and data interpretation, but I'd failed the practical aspect known as Objective Structured Clinical Examinations, or OSCEs. This practical element consisted of 15 stations, divided into two components. Initially you faced ten stations that tested your clinical examination or consultation skills. At each station there would be a given scenario: on one side of the door yourself with a patient/an actor, plus an examiner on the other side. You were required to either examine a patient or take a history from an actor, and then have a discussion with the examiner regarding differential diagnoses and management plans. The other component of the OSCEs was the five clinical skills stations where again scenarios were placed outside rooms and you were then required to perform clinical skills on a variety of prosthetic body parts. They could be any five from the core skills that we were required to be competent in during our clinical training, such as: phlebotomy, cannulation, arterial blood gas sampling, catheterisation and so on. The list is quite lengthy.

Of the 15 stations, you could fail five. I failed six. I knew I'd made a mess of phlebotomy, not because I couldn't bleed the rubber arm, but because the scenario had highlighted that the sample was 'high risk' and, as such, I should have been aware that there was specific labelling required on the pathology form to warn people who subsequently came into contact with it. However, I forgot to attach the red dot label and put it in a high risk bag. I also felt that I could have done better in the IM injection station and the suturing station. But I genuinely found it difficult to understand how I'd failed the cardiovascular and abdominal examinations. I was invited by the Deanery to attend a debrief that afternoon, where it would be explained where I'd gone wrong and what would happen next.

During this chat, which in the long run proved to be very helpful, I was allowed to review the mark sheets for the stations that I'd failed. For both the cardiology and abdominal stations, the examiner in the room that day had given me a score that indicated a clear pass. When I queried this it was explained to me that it was not that simple. To be honest, I was still a bit numb, I tried to take it all in but I'm still not sure that I fully understood how the system worked, but I think I get the principle. Because not all candidates can be assessed by the same examiner, there will be a variation in the scores achieved, and therefore in order to try and maintain a level playing field for all candidates, all the results of all the candidates are put through a statistical analysis formula to establish a uniform pass mark. When this model was applied, mine came out below the cut-off point.

I was, shall we say, somewhat bewildered and disappointed. It seemed that I'd failed medicine via the Duckworth-Lewis method!

But I also knew that I just had to take it on the chin and resit them. All my mates had passed their exams and were now doctors. I went to see them in a pub on North Road, to congratulate them on their incredible achievement, and wish them the best for their futures. The thing is, the course is so attritional that it engenders an incredible unity, borne out of adversity and mutual respect. We had a few beers and they were, of course, amazingly supportive of me, with many concerned as to how I felt rather than given to their own rejoicing. I reassured them that I was OK, and that I'd get through the resit, and that I was there to enjoy their moment, not dwell on my failure.

This was a time of enormous pressure at home too, because by now Leisha and I were proud parents of Michael and Johnathan, our six-month-old twin boys. They were born on 5 October 2011, a birthday they share with the Warburton twins and Gwyn Jones! Their arrival into the world, a couple of days before Wales beat Ireland in the World Cup, was an absolute joy and delight. Had I passed I would have had time from April until early August to mainly be at home with my family, and help share some of the daily workload that Leisha had been getting through alone. Leisha was, at this stage, effectively a single parent. For eight months she lived 'Groundhog Day'. She is a remarkable mother and ensured that the boys early days weren't adversely affected by my rainbow chasing. I guess the hard truth is that becoming the father of twins six months before the final exams which I sat in the middle of the Six Nations, whilst also still trying to earn a crust as broadcaster to pay the bills and my way through school, I just might have just bitten off more than I could chew. This could not be my story, however, without a LFB element. The year that I failed was the first in which the Deanery allowed resits of finals. Prior to that, failure meant either redoing the entire final year or simply being told to leave altogether. At least I had the chance of a resit before being put back a year or kicked out.

Resits or not, there was still a very real possibility that I might have to pack medicine in. Finding another job at this stage might not have been easy. By now, I was looking like a serial fantasist and wannabe pub owner, restaurateur and broadcaster. After all the sacrifices Leisha had made to support me through college, and with two young babies to look after, I felt a huge weight of responsibility. There was also a very personal issue, in that I'd applied myself to something 100 per cent for the first time in my life, but it looked like I might have come up short. Was this me once again underachieving, but on a greater scale than at any other time in my life?

The pressure built steadily with each minute in the library, the skills lab, or in the sessions laid on by the Deanery. The minutes, hours and days went by until I drove up to Llandough for the resit. It's impossible to describe how I felt that day. The burden of caring and providing for my family, as well as the burden of being made to look like a fool for pursing such an ambitious dream, were heavy, heavy weights indeed. I actually felt that my resit exams went worse than the first time I'd tried them, probably because I knew that I absolutely had to get it right this time. But, I also knew what to expect, and while the patients were going to be a completely different mix, I knew the structure and knew what was required to pass, or fail.

I'd redoubled my efforts in the intervening three months. All my medical pals gave up their time to help me; Gwyn and Marc were willing examination props who could also critique my performance. I never let an opportunity go to waste. The postgraduate team at the Princess of Wales hospital, especially Wendy Davies, helped me out enormously. I would sit in the kitchen with a prosthetic skin block and other bits of kit that Carl and Nick in the clinical skills lab had let me borrow. By the time I resat the clinical skills, my suturing was now of surgical standard and I could pop a cannula in from the other side of the room! Well almost!

So the day came and went, and we had to wait again for the results which came the morning after the 2012 Welsh rugby writers' dinner at Cardiff RFC. Everyone in the room wished me all the best. I stayed out quite late, not due to my usual lust for beer, but because I was afraid to go to bed, because that meant I'd have to get up and check my e-mail in the morning.

The list was shorter this time, but my number was on it! I replied to all texts this time! Jamie Roberts broke the news on Twitter! Serendipity ensured that I'd get that beer with Jamie, as that evening we were the guests of Bettws RFC in Newport, and they treated us like royalty.

With hindsight, the resits helped me and, of course, if I'm honest they were valid. There were question marks over some of my clinical competence and it was necessary to ensure that I was safe. Those three months of extra and intensive training ensured that when I stepped onto the wards in August, I was equipped with the skills required. I was extremely proud to have qualified, even if my confidence had been shaken. But yet again, as was the case so often in my life, I found that I wasn't on my own. I had a team around me, and that team contained Connor and Emily Howorth, fellow F1s (Foundation Year 1), and their support in my first post as an F1 was invaluable.

Our boss on that first rotation in Bridgend was the colorectal surgeon, Mr Barry Appleton. I enjoyed my time working on his team, even though he was younger than me! One of the proudest moments in my life came later that year when Mr Appleton stopped me in the main corridor and asked me, 'What would you say if I told you that I would like to nominate you for the Trust's Foundation Year 1 Doctor of the Year Award?'

'I would ask if you were drunk, Mr Appleton, or if you'd had a blow to the head?'

He laughed, but explained his rationale. 'Clinically, you might not be the best F1 we've ever had, but you are an interesting character. You bring something different to medicine.' It was an incredible boost to hear the things he said, and to hear how he viewed my role as a doctor.

I am a huge advocate – almost evangelical in fact – of graduate entry doctors, for many of the reasons that have been mentioned in passing already. What would I have been able to bring to medicine when I was 18? But, having knocked on doors as a rep or worked behind a bar, you know more about people, about work.

The people I was training with – those mentioned and others I came to know – came from all sorts of interesting backgrounds. Lambers was a physio; Ryan had been a male nurse who wanted to practise medicine in a different way; Connor, with a brain the size of Lansdowne Road, was a chemistry graduate who'd worked in the labs of a pharmaceutical company but wanted more human contact. That is the key here; the massive advantage I feel we had over our undergraduate colleagues was because of our experience of 'life'. That abstract concept is immeasurable, yet invaluable in a highly-pressurised environment such as front-line medicine. Having worked in various industries, it not only makes you appreciate that medicine is a wonderful and privileged career, it gives you invaluable experience of simply dealing with people.

Knowing how to interact with patients, colleagues, and

relatives is extremely important. I'm reasonably competent at patient interaction, but in other aspects I've come to learn that I'm not quite the person that I think I am. Despite my 'experience', I've found out that I don't always deal with situations in quite the way I'd like to think I would. This happens at times of increased pressure, when the jobs generated by the ward round are piling up, when one or two patients are getting sicker, or when you are on-call and your bleep is relentless. Learning how to manage your time, prioritise your workload, and remain professional in your interactions with colleagues is not always as easy as it sounds.

After a lifetime of *almost* achieving something, I probably found it hard to acknowledge when I actually did succeed. Often, since qualifying, people will chat to me about studying medicine and express their admiration. Like so many people, I struggle with the compliments, possibly due to a lack of experience in getting them! As I've already said, if we're speaking at an event together, Steeley will always introduce me as a modest man, given that I have plenty to be modest about!

A question that I'm asked most often is what prompted me to study medicine at that time of life. You'd think that by now I'd have a good answer. The truth is, the more I consider the question, the deeper it takes me. It seems to have ticked so many boxes for me. I think that primarily I have a great job, offering incredible work satisfaction, the ability to help people at a time when they really need it. What could possibly be better than that?

When you become a doctor later in life, you realise how wonderful a job it is. You're not stuck with a decision you thought was a good idea when you were 18, one that you can't get out of years later when you've had enough. Maybe

I took that to a bit of an extreme by not starting until I was 40, I'll admit that! But the point stands.

There are, of course, challenging aspects to the job. The emotional side can often take a heavy toll on me. Throughout my life I'd had little experience of death. My nan died at good age when she was 87, so personal grief was something of a stranger.

In my experience medicine is not much like *Casualty*. Attending cardiac arrest calls and administering CPR is both physically and emotionally draining, and rarely has a positive outcome. Breaking bad news to a family that their loved one has died is a very humbling experience that I've gone through a number of times, and it doesn't get any easier. I'll also be haunted by my time on the ITU at the Heath, when I needed to comfort an old friend whose son had died following a tragic accident. As a father, I simply cannot imagine what he was feeling. I have a massive admiration for the ITU staff; they deal with this every day of their working lives and yet stay focused and achieve, frankly, amazing results.

At the time of writing I've completed my foundation training successfully and I'm now in my first year of the Glamorgan Valleys GP training scheme. At some point, in about three years' time, I'll be sitting in a GP practice somewhere calling patients into my room and I'll be responsible for their care. That will be nine years after I first turned up at medical school.

Now, as I look back on that decision to study medicine, it really was the right thing for me to go for. It has given me a job that I can call my own, whatever else happens in other areas. It also makes me very proud because, as I've said, being a doctor is such a privilege.

18

So, is it all rugby? If you've stuck with the story this far then you might think yes, it is. From birth, through school and college rugby teams, rugby clubs and rugby broadcasting, rugby was the constant. Whether it was forging links that influenced my sales career or owning the Cameo Club, or even my transition into medicine. Rugby has been central to everything I've done and it has given me so much. I'm sure that it always will, I couldn't imagine my life without it. However, this version of my life is the edited highlights, this book is effectively the *Scrum V* of my life!

There have been an awful lot of facets to my life and so it isn't all about rugby either, is it? I'm a doctor now. I'm part of another team that has to deal with situations that are literally matters of life and death. I have privileges and occasions for pride in medicine that rugby cannot give.

And I, most importantly of all, have a family.

Mum brought me up with unquestioning love and devotion. She ensured that I wanted for nothing and if things were ever difficult for her to do so, she never showed me – although she might have mentioned it once or twice since! I had every encouragement and support from her as I started to show an interest in rugby, and she was understanding enough when I followed every single mad pursuit off the field, as well. I'll never be able to repay her, even if she wanted me to.

You've heard a lot about dad and how he has influenced my life despite the geography – perhaps because of the geography. I treasure those times I spent with him and Marlene both in Australia and also on their recent trips here for my marriage to Leisha and my graduation. He may not have been around as much as either of us would have liked, but we have had some fun. More importantly though, through my dad so many great people came into my life, like my Uncle Chris and Auntie Avril.

What drives me on now is that I have a very special family of my own. Leisha and I have just celebrated 20 years as a couple since we met that night at Bosun's Locker; we married on that same date 12 years later. We have come a very long way together, and like all couples we've had some great times and some tough times. Again, it's no exaggeration to say that I simply could not have achieved any of it without her. Leisha supported all my dreams, not just spiritually but often financially.

When your husband, at 38, says: 'Guess what dear, I'm going to give up my well-paid job and car, with pension and healthcare, and go back to school to train to be a doctor' it takes a very special person to say: 'OK, I'm right behind you.'

Leisha's belief in me has been unwavering even as I lurched from what might have seemed one bad idea to another. I cannot imagine having done it all without her love and support.

Our greatest achievements, of course, are Michael and Johnathan, our adorable twins who have opened up a whole new world for me. Having just turned three, they may be twins but they are both so different. Their personalities are now really blossoming, and again I must pay tribute to Leisha who, as a top-class nanny, has found that she has some obviously transferable skills. She is kind, gentle, loving, nurturing and extremely patient, and as a result we are blessed with very happy and well-balanced boys... most of the time!

I cannot wait to watch them grow and develop and see what they make of this wonderful world and the opportunities it throws their way. I hope that they enjoy themselves as much as I do, but perhaps find some true direction a little sooner than I did. Funnily enough I wouldn't be that upset at all if they had no interest in rugby. I just want them to be happy, which again is no newsflash; every father wants this but that doesn't make it any less true.

Suddenly, through the boys, I understand things a bit more, especially what my mum meant when she kept banging on, 'You'll understand when you have children.'

I didn't then. I do now.

So I think I can say that for me it was all rugby, but now there is so much more.

It's All Rugby is just one of a whole range of
publications from Y Lolfa. For a full list of
books currently in print, send now for your
free copy of our new full-colour catalogue.
Or simply surf into our website

www.ylolfa.com

for secure on-line ordering.

y Lolfa

Talybont Ceredigion Cymru SY24 5HE
e-mail ylolfa@ylolfa.com
website www.ylolfa.com
phone (01970) 832 304
fax 832 782